The Early Days of
AVIATION
in
GRAND RAPIDS

The Early Days of

AVIATION

in

GRAND RAPIDS

GORDON G. BELD

THE
History
PRESS

Published by The History Press
Charleston, SC 29403
www.historypress.net

Copyright © 2012 by Gordon G. Beld
All rights reserved

Unless otherwise noted, all images used come from the public domain.

First published 2012

Manufactured in the United States

ISBN 978.1.60949.894.8

Library of Congress CIP data applied for.

For my sister, Peg Hinken,
who has devoted her life
to caring for others.

Contents

Preface

GLANCING BACK AND LOOKING UP

It's now been a little more than a century since we figured out how to do what birds have been doing from the beginning. Flying machines with wings didn't come along until December 17, 1903, when the Wright Brothers got off the ground at Kitty Hawk. Their plane made it into the air for the first time that day, going 852 feet on the last and longest of several flights. A lot has happened since then. We've even been to the moon—and now we're looking beyond that.

For some of us, airplanes may no longer be exceptional. But, for me, there's always been something exciting about seeing—or, better yet, being in—one of those fascinating machines that speed through the clouds.

When I was a kid in the Grand Rapids suburbs, an aviator wasn't what I wanted to be when I grew up. Nevertheless, the sound and sight of early 1930s planes zooming overhead always got my attention. Our Wyoming Township home was just a couple miles northwest of the old Kent County Airport at Madison Avenue and Thirty-second Street, and even in those days, airplanes were almost always in the sky.

First, there were the Ducks—the Keystone-Loening amphibians of Kohler Airlines that looked like the web-footed birds and didn't fly much faster. They carried passengers between Grand Rapids and Milwaukee and usually came right over our house. Then came those big, all-metal Ford Trimotors. The aerial acrobatics of smaller planes were exciting to watch, too—especially the diving and loop-the-looping biplanes. A special treat would be the sight of a skywriting plane that spewed smoke to form letters as the pilot maneuvered.

These photos of a balloon ascension at Holland State Park in the 1930s were among the first taken by the author with his new Kodak Baby Brownie camera. *Author's collection.*

Closer looks at those magnificent machines often came during Sunday afternoons when my dad, George Beld, would drive me out to the edge of the airport where I'd peer through a car window to watch planes take off and land.

Then something even more exciting happened. I was about five years old, and I actually climbed aboard a plane owned by Ben Burkhead. His drugstore, located a block from our home at the corner of Chicago Drive and Nagel Avenue, was the best store ever—the source of comic books, chocolate sodas and those 1930s baseball cards that, for only a penny, came with a piece of gum the same size as the card. As a promotion for the store, Ben offered rides to customers. My Aunt Corra was a bit more daring than my mother, so she went up with me and my cousins, Marshall and Russell Norden. That was the first time I saw the world from up above.

A decade passed before I got a view like that again. I became a soldier a few months after World War II ended and was sent to Germany for occupation duty. Most GIs didn't get to overseas assignments in planes during those days, so my travels were on water rather than in the air. However, when my term of service ended, I needed transportation from Fort Dix, New Jersey, back to Grand Rapids. Trains and buses were slower than I wanted to go, and commercial airfare was more than army pay would permit.

The solution was a trip on a war surplus C-47 transport being used by Air Force veterans to haul freight. On the way to cargo pickups, they'd fly returning GIs to their homes. I was able to get a flight from Teterboro, New Jersey, to Detroit for next to nothing. Taxis and a bus took me the rest of the way. The plane wasn't luxurious. No soft seats. We sat on planks along the sides of the cabin. After we deplaned at Detroit, the C-47 went on to St. Louis and loaded freight for delivery back in the East.

After that, I went up a couple times on Douglas DC-3s, flying into and out of Kent County Airport. But most of my trips aloft came much later—after daughter Dala met a young man in the Basque Country on the north coast of Spain. When grandchildren entered the picture a few years later, transatlantic flights became necessary for spending time with them. Those journeys were aboard today's big jets, mostly Boeing 747s and 757s.

My grandson, Alar Basurko, inherited my love of airplanes, and his efforts to learn all he could about them intensified my interest. When he was a bit older, I was with him at the time he prodded my brother-in-law John Debbink to tell him what it was like to pilot a B-24 Liberator bomber over Europe during World War II. Usually reluctant to talk about that, John opened up and had us on the edges of our chairs.

So, a lot of people—Dad, Ben, Aunt Corra, Dala, Alar, John and others—had a hand in inspiring this book. Of course, my continuing interest in aviation did too. I'm not a kid anymore. But I still look up every time I hear an engine in the sky. And I still find memories and stories of flying in the good old days captivating. It's my hope that the following pages will provide that same kind of fascination for you.

—Gordon G. Beld

Acknowledgements

Without the help of several generous persons and organizations, this book would not have been possible. Tim Gleisner, supervisor of the Local History and Special Collections section of the Grand Rapids Public Library, along with his friendly and helpful aides, found materials and photographs and offered suggestions and encouragement that made research there especially pleasant. Staff members of the Midway Village Museum at Rockford, Illinois, and the Kalamazoo Air Zoo in Michigan generously and quickly responded to requests for photographs. I'm also grateful to a friend of long ago—the late Charles Clapp—who provided my first opportunity to write about the history of Grand Rapids aviation. Editor of the *Grand Rapids Herald* when I was a staff writer there, Charlie asked me to interview and write about pioneer aviator Bert Kenyon. The result was a page-one feature on Sunday, July 28, 1957.

CHAPTER 1

The Start of It All

Even today, it's thrilling to see a plane zoom overhead or a hot-air balloon float past. But imagine the excitement such a sight would bring to someone who'd never seen anything but a bird, bat or bug doing that.

At Grand Rapids, the first time there was something else up there in the sky was Independence Day 1859. In its next edition, the *Grand Rapids Eagle* proclaimed, "The 'glorious 4th' was the occasion of the most remarkable and the largest congregation of people here ever known in the history of this city."

The main reason for the crowd and all the excitement was a scheduled balloon ascension. Professor William D. Bannister—that's what they called the daring fliers in those days—was bringing his big bag and actually would go up in the air.

Previous celebrations of the Fourth at the banks of Grand River had been rather tame. The earliest was in 1834, a year after the first permanent settlers arrived. That year most of the newcomers paraded down an Indian trail. "They marched up the trail and down and about," early historian Charles Baxter wrote, "and sang and shouted, and fiddled and hurrahed. Many Indians joined in the sport."

Three years later, the first of the Grand River steamboats was the big attraction of the July holiday. The day's oration was delivered from the deck of the *Governor Mason*. During three Independence Days in the early 1840s, cruises down the river to Grandville and back on the steamer *Paragon* were the Independence Day highlights.

After that, for several years, there were no sensational happenings on the Fourth. Then Bannister came to town with his big balloon, *Pride of America.* "As early as four o'clock in the morning," the *Eagle* reported, "a stream of wagons, from all parts of the country, began to pour into the city. By sunrise, and until early noon, all the principal avenues leading into town were crowded with vehicles of every description, all moving toward a principal center of attraction—the public square." Today, that's Campau Square at the heart of downtown.

Crowds also came by boat and by train. The steamboat *Michigan*, with three hundred aboard, arrived at nine in the morning; and at ten-thirty an excursion train discharged a thousand passengers from the Lowell area at the depot. The *Eagle* estimated there were fifteen thousand visitors in the city.

Though some of them may have heard that Bannister ascended from Bronson Park at Kalamazoo a month earlier, most probably knew little about him. In 1854, he soared 350 miles with a passenger aboard from Adrian in southeastern Michigan to Clarion, Pennsylvania, where both men were found unconscious in the balloon basket, which was tangled in a tree.

Many of Bannister's later ascensions were made in partnership with Ira Thurston. During autumn 1858, they lifted off from Adrian and descended on a farm at nearby Ogden, a rather uneventful flight. But, after Bannister got out to disengage ropes and weights, the balloon, with Thurston in it, suddenly shot up again—"like a rocket," bystanders said.

The empty balloon was found later at West Tilbury, Canada, but there was no sign of Thurston until the following spring when his remains, just scattered bones, were found at Sylvania, a Toledo suburb. Identification was made from scraps of clothing and a letter addressed to the balloonist.

Thurston's adopted daughter, Nellie—known as the Queen of Cloudland— also flew balloons from Adrian. Before a divorce, she was married to John LaMountain, a balloonist who later performed at Grand Rapids.

The day before Bannister's 1859 flight, the *Eagle* warned its Grand Rapids readers that "no fireworks or other combustibles must be burned in the vicinity of the balloon enclosure. The balloon is to be inflated with common gas, and the consequences of setting it on fire might be disastrous in the extreme."

At midafternoon on the Fourth, roofs of downtown buildings became crowded with those who wanted a view from slightly above the launch site. It was nearly five o'clock when the balloon lifted and began to slip off to the west. It eventually landed three miles from its departure point.

"The day was remarkably clear and pleasant," the *Eagle* reported, "and all the motions of the balloon and its occupant were plainly visible until it had sunk, in its descent, below the tops of the trees. Shortly before sundown the balloon was seen returning into town, still two-thirds inflated and attached to a wagon. It was taken back to the square and relieved of its contents."

In 1863, while many Grand Rapids men were off fighting on Civil War battlefields, the city's Independence Day activities were based at Island Number One in Grand River near the Pearl Street Bridge. On that day, according to historian Baxter, an ascension was made from the island by a balloonist named Ayeres.

The next balloon to fly over the city was the *Comet*, flown by John LaMountain on July 4, 1870. The ascension, the *Grand Rapids Eagle* reported, was made from "the locality at the foot of Justice and Fulton Street, near the gas works." The paper said that nearby hills and the rooftops of all nearby houses were crowded with people who wanted a good look as the balloon was filled and then ascended.

"As the *Comet* majestically arose from the earth," the *Daily Morning Democrat* said, "the huzzas from thousands of voices greeted the ears of the intrepid navigator of the air, who, with gracious smiles and bows, and waving of his handkerchief, acknowledged the compliment as he was lifted by the breeze above the clouds, and was soon a mere speck in the heavens."

The balloon sailed southeast and, thirty-five minutes later, landed in a tamarack swamp on the Cascade Township farm of John Foster (at today's junction of Cascade Road and Spaulding Avenue).

LaMountain was the best known of three balloonist brothers. One of the others, Edward, was killed when his hot-air balloon deflated and plunged to the ground at Ionia on the Fourth of July in 1873.

John, too, had an accident in Michigan but survived. At Bay City a year before he came to Grand Rapids, an impatient crowd let go the ropes holding the balloon before he was ready to take off. Much of his equipment remained on the ground, and the valve soon froze shut so that he could not release gas to descend. He then crawled out of the basket, climbed up to the balloon and reached for his knife. However, it had been left behind, so he tore a hole in the bag with a hand and his teeth. Unable to control the rate the gas escaped, the balloon dropped speedily from a height of two miles. The deflated balloon acted a bit like a parachute, slightly slowing the downward plunge. LaMountain was found lying in a woods, unconscious and bruised but with no broken bones or internal injuries.

Ten years earlier, he joined John Wise in a plan to fly across the Atlantic, but the partnership dissolved after the balloon was badly damaged in a test flight from St. Louis to Henderson, New York. LaMountain kept the balloon, the *Atlantic*, and used it in observation flights for the Union army during the Civil War. His first time aloft for that purpose was on July 31, 1861, and three days later, he made the first balloon ascension from a boat, the Union tug *Fanny*.

However, LaMountain's quarrelsome nature and a struggle with Thaddeus Lowe for the position of chief aeronaut of the Union army soon ended his military career. After Lowe obtained the leadership role, LaMountain did all he could to discredit him. When the controversy became public and threatened morale of Union balloonists, General George McClellan terminated LaMountain's service.

Perhaps the most-publicized flight in the history of ballooning over Grand Rapids was the one by Washington H. Donaldson on July 5, 1875. He took four newspaper reporters up with him, and all of them penned lengthy accounts of their experiences in the next editions of their papers—the *Eagle*, *Times*, *Democrat* and *Saturday Evening Post*. The *Post* wasn't the national magazine; it was a Grand Rapids weekly paper.

The flight of the balloon, the *P.T. Barnum*, was a sideline attraction of Barnum's "Great Roman Hippodrome." The extravaganza was described in an *Eagle* advertisement as "a historical and traditional revelation of the past thousand years." The ad said there'd be "an army of men, women, and children; hundreds of thoroughbred and imported horses; a long and glittering line of gilt and silver besprinkled chariots and tableau cars; countless suits of burnish silver and jeweled armor." There also would be elephant and camel races, as well as an English stag hunt with three hundred horse riders and fifty-two hounds. Music would be provided by "Prof Hartman's Silver Cornet and Reed Band of 50 Musicians, the largest traveling musical organization ever completed."

The balloon was launched from the Front Street site of the gigantic hippodrome tent, which, according to the ad, required "nearly ten acres of wide spread canvas."

Donaldson often went up in crowded balloons. A year earlier, at a New York building that later became Madison Square Garden, he carried five passengers. Later that year at Cincinnati, he took up a wedding party for a ceremony that was performed in the air. And, less than two weeks before the Grand Rapids flight, he went up with three reporters at Toronto and sailed out over Lake Ontario. The balloon came down in the lake, and they were dragged several miles before they were rescued.

Just nine days after his appearance in Grand Rapids, Donaldson went up in Chicago with a single passenger. There were to have been two—Newton

S. Grimwood of the *Chicago Evening Journal* and James Maitland of the *Chicago Post & Mail*. Both were in the basket with Donaldson and ready to go, but the pilot decided he could only take one.

Maitland flipped a coin, said he had won and told Grimwood to get out of the basket. But Donaldson's agent intervened and advised that the decision needed to be made by drawing lots and that he had to be in charge. He took the hat of a policeman standing nearby and placed two slips of paper in it, shook them thoroughly and asked the officer to draw one. Grimwood's name was on it.

In a conversation with a comrade, Grimwood remarked, "I only care to go once, just for the experience." When his friend noted that the wind was unfavorable, Grimwood responded, "I guess they're trying to frighten us by saying Donaldson expects to be carried into Michigan, with the chances of being gone two or three days." In the next breath, he added, "That's what I hope. I would like to land in Michigan. But I guess I ought to have a little more money if I'm going so far from home." His friend handed him a ten-dollar bill.

When the balloon went up, it floated slowly to the northeast and out over Lake Michigan. The crowd on shore peered into the distance, but darkness soon blotted out the image. A schooner, *Little Guide*, about thirty miles offshore and a dozen miles north of Chicago, sighted the balloon and reported the basket occasionally dipped into the lake. The ship headed toward the balloon, but before it could get there, the aircraft rocketed upward and out of view of the sailors below.

No trace of the balloon or either of its occupants could be found. Finally, a month later, a mail carrier, A. Beckwith, was walking the Michigan shoreline seven miles south of Little Point Sable Lighthouse and came across the remains of a body. Papers in the tattered clothing revealed it was Grimwood. Among them were a few notes he had written during the flight.

"I cannot help reflecting," he said in one, "that if we fall, we fall, like Lucifer, out of the heavens, and that our arrival upon earth, or rather upon water—for we are over the middle of Lake Michigan—we would be literally DEAD."

A report in *Inter-Ocean*, a Chicago publication, said that Beckwith turned the remains over to J.J. Tapley, a Claybanks Township justice of the peace who consulted friends and then had Grimwold's remains interred at "Claybanks Cemetery." There is no record of a cemetery with that name in the area, but today's Pine Grove Cemetery has tombstones with 1800s dates and is located less than a mile from the shoreline where Grimwold's remains were

Horses carry their riders along the Lake Michigan shoreline seven miles south of Little Pointe Sable Lighthouse in Oceana County, where the remains of reporter Newton S. Grimwood were found a month after he and balloonist Washington H. Donaldson disappeared after ascending at Chicago. *Author's collection.*

Balloonist Hiram Cole was warned by management of the pavilion here at North Park, alongside the Grand River north of Grand Rapids, not to ascend in his balloon because the wind was too strong. But he felt he needed to go up to fulfill his contract. When he did, he was knocked from his trapeze and killed.

found by Beckwith. Records for this cemetery have no listing for Grimwold, so if he was buried there, the remains probably were exhumed and taken by relatives to the Chicago area.

Neither Donaldson nor the balloon was ever found.

Before the end of the nineteenth century, tragedy struck in Grand Rapids, too. Balloonist Hiram Cole of Big Rapids was completing a week of ascensions at North Park in late June 1896. He had gone up on Sunday, June 21, and again the following Wednesday. He'd fulfill his contract obligations with another Sunday flight. It turned out to be an exceptionally windy day; and Frank Potter, manager of the park pavilion, advised him not to go up.

After the Wednesday flight, according to the *Grand Rapids Herald*, Potter's wife "cautioned the flier to always be careful. He had replied that his life was at stake and that he would surely take care always."

Cole realized the ascension would be difficult, but he felt he needed to satisfy his contract. So he went up, hanging below the balloon on a trapeze, and had gone only thirty feet before he was knocked off. He landed on his head and shoulders and was carried to the pavilion by some in the crowd. A doctor at the nearby Michigan Soldiers Home was summoned, but Cole died without regaining consciousness.

For many years, balloon ascensions drew large crowds to another popular entertainment attraction, Ramona Park at the shore of Reeds Lake in East Grand Rapids. Two female balloonists were among those who went up late in the nineteenth century and in the early twentieth. The first was a young lady whom the *Grand Rapids Evening Leader* identified as "Miss Nellie Lamonte."

She probably was Nellie LaMountain, the wife of John. In various publications, her name also was said to be "LaMonte," "LaMont," and "LaMonunt." At birth she was Ellen Moss, and when she was adopted by balloonist Ira Thurston, she became Nellie Thurston. John LaMountain was said by some to be her cousin and, by others, an uncle sixteen years her senior. They divorced in 1865, and in 1871, Nellie began ballooning with Howard D. Squires, who had begun his aerial activities as a partner of LaMountain.

Nellie and Howard married soon after they met. In 1874 at Brockville, Ontario, he suffered severe injuries when his balloon tangled with a church steeple and the basket crashed into the building. He gave up ballooning and, when he recovered, served as Nellie's manager. She was the first woman to go aloft in a balloon over Canada, where many of her ascensions eventually were made.

She also flew frequently in the northern United States, and in an 1878 flight from Oneida, New York, she took along a homing pigeon. She opened

Crowds sometimes filled the shoreline of Reeds Lake at Ramona Park in East Grand Rapids to watch balloon ascensions and races. Two female balloonists who went up at Ramona needed to be rescued. One landed in the lake and the other in a tree, where she was suspended for more than three hours.

the cage at an altitude of three miles, but the bird wouldn't fly. When she put it on the edge of the basket, it jumped down to the floor. She set it on the edge again, and it flipped to her shoulder. When she tossed it out into the air, it flew around the balloon a few times and came back to the basket. She picked it up, gave it a kiss and the bird flew out of her hand and out of sight. The balloon was back at Oneida a day before the bird.

At Ramona Park on September 21, 1890, five thousand watched as Nellie ascended at 5:00 p.m. and soared out over Reeds Lake. Her parachute drop from the airship went fine, except she landed in the lake and had to be rescued by crewmen and passengers aboard the park's steamboat.

The *Herald*'s account of the day's activities gave more space to trolley transportation to and from the park than it did to Nellie's flight. According to the paper, derailment of an outgoing streetcar blocked one coming in that had 128 people aboard and hanging from it. Passengers had to help lift the derailed car back onto the track to alleviate the problem, and in the confusion, some of them got on the wrong cars.

The next lady to fly at Ramona, Mrs. Blanche Baxter, also needed to be rescued when her balloon landed. She was a local resident and, according to the *Grand Rapids Press*, was making her first ascension in July 1916. "She substituted for Anomar, the young woman balloonist whom Henry Phelps sent to Benton Harbor to make a flight," the *Press* said.

When she parachuted from the balloon, she missed the lake but crashed into a pine tree, where she was stranded for nearly four hours. Ted King, a lineman for the Grand Rapids Railway Company, was recruited to free her. However, the belt he used for climbing was too short to go around the tree. As the would-be rescuers pondered how to solve the problem, she frequently called down to tell them she was all right and to take their time. Eventually, with the use of ropes, she was lowered to safety.

With the development of heavier-than-air flying machines early in the twentieth century, the fascination of balloon ascensions began to dim. However, the silent, smoothly floating air vessels still draw scores of balloonists and thousands of spectators to colorful festivals such as those each year at Battle Creek. And, for most of us, even the sight of a single balloon sailing past is enough to bring a halt to whatever we're doing while we follow its flight until it fades out of sight.

CHAPTER 2

How Things Looked
from Up There

All four of the Grand Rapids reporters who went along with Washington Donaldson for a ride over Grand Rapids in 1875 dug deep and pulled out what they thought were their best words for sharing their impressions of the balloon flight.

The Independence Day extravaganza actually took place on July 5 since the Fourth was a Sunday that year. The trip started at the huge hippodrome tent, where one of Phineas T. Barnum's extravaganzas was thrilling crowds, and it ended on a farm in Ada Township. Each of the writers, of course, had his own style. But none of the others could match the word-cramming talent of the *Eagle*'s Robert Wilson, who packed ninety-one of them into the first sentence of his story:

> *Yesterday was the Fourth, although the Fifth, and the usual amount of hard work which falls to the lot of a daily newspaper reporter, in keeping track of the crowd that passed in endless throngs through the streets, on the lookout for fights, frights, accidents and incidents was ours; trudging along over sidewalks and pavements, through clouds of dust and into the thick of miniature mobs, ever on the alert for "something to turn up," while the thermometer had turned up above the nineties, and was almost boiling in the shade.*

Readers who waded through that may have found the rest of his report informative and entertaining. After the babbling account of the tough life of a newsman in hot weather, Wilson did actually get to the story of his balloon ride. The others did so in shorter fashion. Following are excerpts from the reports of each of them.

SID F. STEVENS

Grand Rapids Saturday Evening Post

After some preliminary maneuvers, the gallant Prof. Donaldson gave the word, "Let go," and P.T. Barnum, at just 4 p.m., taking an easterly direction, ascended majestically amidst the acclamations of at least thirty thousand people. When at an altitude of 300 feet, Prof. Donaldson, who was just above the reporters on a wire screen, gave orders to them to commence and let out the drag rope. This rope was about 300 feet long and one inch in diameter, so for about fifteen minutes it was pretty busy times in that basket. We were cautioned by the professor to be careful while doing this as, if we were not and should let go of the rope, instead of communing with the angels it would be otherwise...

I never before, and never expect again, to witness so fine and beautiful a sight as the earth then presented, for we could see at least one hundred miles, north, south, east, and west as easily as you can see one mile below. Hastings, Ada, Lowell, Greenville, Lansing, Jackson, Grand Haven, Kalamazoo, and many other places were all visible. Grand River would be followed mile by mile until it passed into Lake Michigan, which seemed to be one mammoth sheet of glass. Nearly every lake and stream over which we passed, to all appearances, was as clear as crystal, and often the bottom could be seen. The state house at Lansing was distinctly visible, and all this with the naked eye, as none of us had thought to provide a glass of any description.

The sound of voices did not seem to reach us, but at one time a peculiar noise was heard, which came from the north; and Bob insisted that it must be at Cedar Springs as he knew who the orator was who had been engaged to speak that day. We could not believe it, but when he told us who it was we concluded he must be right.

ED. J. CLARK

Grand Rapids Democrat

The word was passed to let her off, and up we started, the band playing "Up in a Balloon." And away she went, up, up, slowly, surely, majestically, up, until we thought we should ascend as high as did Elijah in his chariot of fire. A little more up, and then the strong cool breeze of an easterly current caught us, and wafted us in the direction of Detroit.

Down many hundred feet, if not more, was the hot air which made us puff a few moments before, while that around us was getting icy, and we began to yearn for our overcoats. The hippodrome tent looked like a buckwheat cake on a gridiron; and the elephants, basking in the river, resembled, in size, flies…

To try and tell what we saw and describe the beauties which surrounded us is more than we, or the four of us, can successfully do. If the Mohamadan's paradise is beautiful, and Eden lovely, then this scene must have been "more so." The earth seemed one vast plain, dotted with the green patches of emerald hue, with forty lakes of the clearest water, and on the banks of these lakes could be seen rows of young farms—and young onions. Sid claimed that he could see potato bugs waltzing on the potato vines, and called our attention to it; but, although we could not see them waltz, we could hear them walk. Grand River looked like a tape worm, winding its way to Lake Michigan, the great receiving reservoir or stomach of the tape worms of Michigan…

While directly over the Detroit & Milwaukee Railroad, the excursion train en route eastward saw us and stopped, and the passengers came out of the cars and gave us the usual handkerchief flirtation, which was highly appreciated by us. The train resembled the toy train we once found in our stocking, placed there by our paternal relative years ago on Christmas morning.

Robert Wilson

Grand Rapids Daily Eagle

The dimensions of the vast crowd around the hippodrome tent, which extended over acres when we started, had been gradually contracting and narrowing, until now it seemed but a black spot about the size and shape of a wheelbarrow; Grand River shrunk up until its banks nearly touched each other, and resembled a crooked piece of bright wire in a setting of Paris Green; the reservoir was a glass eye set in a circular chunk of mud, and the rapids were strewn thick with matches instead of saw logs.

Men dwarfed to pigmies an inch in height; buildings and long rows of blocks grew small, smaller, and resembled old-fashioned chicken coops; the city huddled itself into the size of Rockford; but the country opened out vast and broad, stretching away flat and level as a floor. Forests were asparagus beds…

Away to the westward we traced the river, which grew wider as its distance increased from us until it was a broad case knife, and upon its point a large, bright tin platter which was Lake Michigan. Grand Rapids seemed a village; Rockford, away to the northward, was increased to twice its size, and Plainfield enlarged fast, all the farm buildings around it waltzing gracefully together. Ada, Lowell, Saranac, Ionia, Greenville, Grandville, and other places were plainly in view; and each of them was larger than the city of 35,000 inhabitants we had just left.

Reeds Lake was just the size and shape of a small bath tub, and its sailboats strangely resembled the moths, or millers, that flutter around the gas light summer evenings. Black spots, about the size of a flyspeck, were seen on toothpicks floating on its surface, and these were the brawny Scotchmen, pulling around in boats of eighteen and twenty-two feet keel.

F.F. JEFFRIES

Grand Rapids Daily Morning Times

Prof. Donaldson's balloon came down at 5:30 last evening, just over the town line of Grand Rapids in Ada. The balloon contained 75,000 cubic feet of gas and sailed away majestically, immediately rising to a distance of over one half mile. The balloon then took an easterly course over Reeds Lake and Saddle Bag Swamp, and finally folded itself up in the woods about three miles from the village of Ada. Large numbers of people followed the balloon for two miles, and when the aerial monster ended its journey about forty persons were present to assist in folding it up.

An attempt was made to effect a landing by means of the guy rope which caught in a tree, and the Professor was compelled to cut loose from it. Shortly after, a rope was thrown out, which the farmers grasped and drew the balloon from the woods into a meadow, where the excursionists and Prof. Donaldson disembarked. A team was chartered, which brought the party into the city, arriving about 9 o'clock...

To attempt a description of the beauties of the earth as viewed from above is not within the power of man. If the garden of Eden was half as beautiful, it must have been extremely lovely. The earth looked like one vast plain, rich with the greenest verdure, with beautiful lakes of the clearest water dotting it here and there. Rivers that looked like a silver thread ran through the vast expanse, while cities and villages could be seen on every side. Soon after leaving the circus grounds, Lake Michigan's broad expanse became visible, looking as calm and undisturbed as a picture...

When near the Detroit & Milwaukee Railroad, the trains of which seemed to be mere toys and moving very slow, they were stopped and the people came out and gave the aerial voyagers the loudest cheers, which were easily heard. The shrill whistle of the locomotive also greeted them.

CHAPTER 3

A Nice Try

It sounded too good to be true. Grand Rapids residents soon would be seeing an airplane soaring overhead, and it would be one that was manufactured right in their city—at a carpet sweeper factory, no less.

These magnificent flying machines had been produced elsewhere, but by 1910, none of them had yet flown above West Michigan. Now, however, two local men set out to change that. One of them was Irving J. Bissell, son of the founders of Bissell Carpet Sweeper Company, Melville and Anna Bissell. The other was Frank Mason, the company's master mechanic.

Irving was a clerk in the company that his parents had founded, somewhat by accident, about thirty years before. In the mid-1800s Melville and Anna had a crockery shop in Grand Rapids, and cleaning up the sawdust used for packing was a frustrating problem for Anna. So Melville designed and built a floor-sweeping machine. Customers who saw it wanted to know where they could get one. The Bissell Carpet Sweeper was patented in 1876, and a factory to produce them in quantity was erected in 1883. Melville died in 1889, and Anna took over supervision of operations—making her one of America's first female corporate executives.

During a trip to Europe in 1909, Irving was in Germany when Orville Wright demonstrated one of his planes for the Kaiser. When he returned to the United States, he asked his mother for permission to attempt construction of a plane that might be the forerunner of a new line of business for the Bissell company. She gave him the go-ahead, but with the stipulation that he himself wouldn't fly it.

The first airplane manufactured in Grand Rapids was produced by Irving Bissell and Frank Mason in 1910 at the Bissell Carpet Sweeper Factory. This postcard showing the factory on the bank of Grand River and the advertisement showing the company's principal product were printed at that time.

The *Grand Rapids Press*, at least, seemed satisfied that young Bissell had the talent needed to make the aircraft a reality. "He has witnessed many flights," the paper said, "and made a study of aviation with the intention of one day piloting his own flier [despite what he may have promised his mother]. He is perhaps one of the most expert of the city's gentleman auto drivers and is a natural mechanic."

When planning began, Bissell expected to purchase an engine. Mason, however, said he could make a better one than could be bought. The one Mason produced, Bissell said, "had many clever features. It was a four-cylinder make of an overhead valve type. We had to fit aluminum jackets, over the heads of the cylinders to give us compression, and our main difficulty consisted in making those tight.

"We built the engine right in the plant," Bissell continued, "and ran into so many minor difficulties we almost gave the thing up many times."

However, it was good enough to make a big impression on motor experts. The *Press* noted in a June 4, 1910, report:

The few practical automobile men who have looked over the engine pronounce it the prettiest bit of gas motor design workmanship they have yet seen. It will weigh just 175 pounds, but with cylinders of four-and-one-half inches diameter against a five-inch stroke, promises forty horsepower at conservative rating. It is a valve-in-the-head type of motor, and this is promised to increase the power considerably. This will put the proportion of power to weight about one horsepower to every pound. The water jackets are of aluminum, as is the crank case and every bit of metal whose work will permit the use of aluminum or alloy.

The *Press* story also praised the balancing mechanism of the Bissell-Mason plane, pointing out that it is an application of auxiliary propellers at the tips of the wings, arranged so that upward or downward thrust can right the machine if it shows a tendency to dip or capsize. However, this idea was eventually abandoned.

Planes that were successfully flown at that time had wings covered with fabric, but for greater strength, Bissell and Mason used two thicknesses of cedar veneer glued together. The biplane under construction in the carpet sweeper factory had a wingspan of thirty-four feet.

The frame, according to the *Press* report, was one "by which the designer expects to gain a rigidity and lightness never before attempted in a flying machine.

"This, coupled with the extreme lightness of the motor and its promise of great power and efficient cooling and ignition," the article said, "would indicate that the Bissell flier will be a success."

Nevertheless, all the problems hadn't been ironed out. One of them concerned the landing gear. At first, they tried to launch the plane from a track, at that time a common practice, but a preflight test ruled that out. They tried skids made of spruce, too, but ended up using small bicycle wheels for the landing gear.

The Bissell-Mason machine wasn't yet airworthy by midyear, but at least it looked like an airplane and was exhibited at the 1910 Berlin Fair in Marne.

In November, it was said to be ready for flight tests, and it was disassembled and taken to the farm of J.H. Bonnell near Reeds Lake, where the flight would be made from a half-mile racetrack on the property. The pilots would be Arthur Rosenthal and Frank Lemon.

Neither had flown before—and probably had never seen another airplane. They were well known in the area as "Rose and Lemon," a popular trick bicycle and motorcycle duo. For the climax of their acts, Lemon raced a motorcycle around the inside of a large mesh ball known as the "Globe of Death."

The *Press* said that Rosenthal "has been making a study of aviation, has attended meetings, and received instruction from some of the best birdmen in the business"—but didn't name any of them. "His balancing work," the article continued, "especially qualifies him for aeroplaning and, added to this, his experience in handling motorcycle engines will be of inestimable value in the ticklish game of guiding and controlling the machine."

Despite the inexperience of the pilots, success was anticipated. The newspaper report proclaimed:

> *This plane is to be used as a demonstrator, and if it makes as good as it seems to promise, Grand Rapids will have a regular aeroplane factory turning out both biplanes and monoplanes. It already is assured that the new machine will make a try for the $25,000 prize for the New York-Chicago flight just as soon as Mr. Rose masters its control. There seems little doubt that one of these days in the near future Grand Rapids folk will look up and see a man bird maneuvering above them. And it will be a strictly home production.*

There could be little doubt that the machine would soon be in the air. The engine couldn't be better, according to the *Press*, which quoted Mason after tests were performed. "It developed power even beyond his wildest dreams," the paper said, "and runs so smoothly and economically as to astonish motor experts. The engine is said to be the most powerful machine of its weight and type in existence and shows a full fifty horsepower on the brake."

And the rest of the aircraft was sensational, too, according to the *Press*. "The Bissell-Mason machine," the paper claimed, "is said, by those competent to judge, to be the most perfectly finished airplane in existence. The few aviators who have seen it make this assertion and say also there is no doubt it will fly."

At dawn on the morning of the big test in November 1910, Bissell and Mason roared out to the Bonnell farm in Bissell's Chadwick racing car. But the plane wasn't working as well as the car. Several problems unfolded—one of them the separation of the propeller from its shaft.

After the propeller was properly installed, they returned and tried again. This time, according to the *Press*, "A faulty turnbuckle in one of the steel guy cables pulled out while the machine was supported on blocks in its big tent…This threw an unaccustomed strain on the skids at the rear and the light timber broke. At the same time the forks for the rear set of wheels gave way."

Bissell and Mason repaired the skids and decided to proceed without the rear wheels. Several members of a crowd of about a hundred, who had gathered to see the first plane take off from Grand Rapids, helped to move the machine into position.

At three o'clock that afternoon, Rosenthal climbed into the pilot's seat and the motor was started. The plane moved slowly, friction of the skids at the rear preventing acceleration. After it moved about a hundred feet, a release for the landing wheels broke, and one side of the aircraft dropped down and bent the axle.

Though Bissell and Mason made many attempts to get the plane off the ground—even later off Reeds Lake when it was covered with ice—they were unsuccessful. According to one of the *Press* reports, Bissell had said that in the event of failure, the engine would be used in an "air wagon," which was described as a light road vehicle propelled by fans or a propeller. But he eventually sold the whole machine.

"I guess it was a good thing that we never did get it to fly," Bissell said later, "as someone undoubtedly would have been killed. Frank Lemon and Art Rose were acting as would-be aviators, and neither one of them had ever been off the ground in such a machine. They intended to figure out the manipulation of the thing after they were in the air."

CHAPTER 4

First to Zoom over the City

Folks in Grand Rapids knew about airplanes before 1911, but no one had seen one of those magnificent flying machines in the air above the city until September of that year. That's when pilot J. Clifford Turpin of the Wright Brothers' Exhibition Team came to the West Michigan State Fair at Comstock Park.

After their first successful flight at Kitty Hawk, North Carolina, in 1903, Wilbur and Orville Wright were not enthusiastic about getting into stunt flying and exhibitions, which they referred to as the "mountebank business"—selling quack medicine from a platform. But by 1909, when the Wright Company was founded, they realized exhibitions could add to their income. A team was recruited and trained, then sent around the country to demonstrate this fascinating new kind of transportation.

Turpin arrived in Grand Rapids on Monday, September 11, 1911, a day after his mechanics came to the city and started getting the plane in shape. The aircraft was the new Model B, the first Wright plane to be produced in quantity. It was twenty-six feet long, had a wingspan of thirty-nine feet and used wheels rather than skids. A pusher type plane with the prop pointed to the rear, it had two seats at the leading edge of the lower wing, one for the pilot and one for a passenger.

In describing the aircraft at the fairground in Comstock Park, the *Grand Rapids Herald* said:

J. Clifford Turpin, one of the Wright Exhibition Team pilots, was the first flier to soar over the city of Grand Rapids. *Courtesy of Library of Congress.*

> *The airplane was stared at in amazement yesterday by hundreds who crowded into the tent to catch, in most cases, their first glimpse of the type of vehicle of which so much has recently been said and written. On terra firma, the engine dead, the device is innocent enough. One's first impression is the biplane is a maze of fine wires strung taut here, there, and everywhere…The planes [wings] of this machine are unique in that they carry the signatures of thousands of persons who chose this novel scheme of placing their name on high. It would appear that everywhere the machine had been sent for exhibition purposes, the crowds had grasped the opportunity to inscribe their names on the canvas.*

The first time anyone in Grand Rapids saw a plane overhead was the opening day of the fair, when Turpin took off into a stiff thirty-mile-an-hour wind. He soon zoomed over the Leonard Street Bridge at seven hundred feet, turned and headed back. All in the crowd below were amazed.

In its report of the day's flight, the *Grand Rapids Press* referred to an earlier attempt to fly over the city:

First to Zoom over the City

Grand Rapids has seen its first aeroplane in flight. The first heavier than air machine to soar over the city was one of the biplanes designed by the Wright brothers. To those who witnessed Bud Mars's failure to fly only a little more than a year ago, the businesslike manner in which aviator Clifford Turpin took up his Wright machine yesterday afternoon, in a wind that was higher and more gusty than the breeze which kept Mars and his Curtiss aeroplane on the ground, made a distinct impression. A few, who witnessed the failure of the Curtiss plane to make a flight just before the 1910 race meet, expressed a belief that Turpin would not attempt to fly.

The following day, Turpin flew twice, and on the second flight, newspaperman J.E. Worthington was aboard as a passenger. After taking off, Turpin circled the fairground and then headed for Grand Rapids. He again turned at Leonard Street and began to follow the river. About a mile north of the Ann Street Bridge, the engine stopped and the plane dived toward the ground. When it disappeared behind trees, many in the crowd at the fair thought this was just another of the thrills the aviator had planned. But the aircraft failed to reappear, and the worst was feared.

Turpin's mechanics jumped into an automobile and headed to the area where the plane had last been seen. Turpin was reported to have climbed off the airplane with a laugh, assisted his frightened passenger to the ground and then set about cleaning a faulty spark plug. He managed to restart the engine, but not wanting to risk taking off again with a passenger, he left Worthington, who found other transportation back to the fair. The pilot did get airborne, but the engine wasn't at full power, so he landed again. His mechanics arrived at that point and put in a new spark plug. This time, Turpin was able to make it back to the fairground.

Members of the Wright Exhibition Team thrilled crowds throughout the country with aerial exhibitions like Turpin's at Comstock Park. When the Wright brothers finally decided that exhibitions of their planes might be a good idea, they hired Roy Knabenshue to recruit and train a team of fliers.

A builder and flier of dirigibles, Knabenshue had been the first airman to appear at the West Michigan State Fair. That was in 1907, four years before Turpin flew the Wright brothers' heavier-than-air machine over Grand Rapids. In its final report of the 1907 fair activities, the *Herald* noted that the five thousand persons who saw the aircraft's last flight at

The fairground at Comstock Park looked like this in 1911 when Clifford Turpin's flights were the big attractions. After a six-year run of the Michigan State Fair at this site ended with its move to the east side of the state in 1901, West Michigan began using the fairground for its own state fair.

Theodore Roosevelt became the first former president to fly when he went up with Wright flier Archibald Hoxsey in 1910. Another Roosevelt, Franklin D., was the first to ride in a plane while serving as president. That was thirty-three years later, when he flew to the Casablanca Conference. *Courtesy of Library of Congress.*

Comstock Park "were more than satisfied that navigation of the air can be accomplished."

Knabenshue and his dirigible were back at the fairground two years later with Lincoln Beachey, who soon gave up flying the gas-filled airships and became one of the country's best-known pioneer airplane pilots.

At the 1909 fair, Knabenshue commented on the increasing popularity of heavier-than-air machines. "The whole public is simply crazy to see airplane exhibitions," he said, "and I predict that next year will see the temporary end of the dirigible balloon exhibition. It will only be temporary though. The aeroplanes with their great spread of wings are unsafe when the slightest current of air is stirring."

After the first members of the Wright Exhibition Team had been recruited by Knabenshue and received flight training from Orville Wright, the group's first public appearance was at the Indianapolis Motor Speedway on June 13, 1910. A year earlier, Carl Fisher, builder of the speedway, had nine balloons from throughout the nation at the track for the first national balloon race. The 1910 event was described as the "first licensed aviation meet in the U.S." The big appeal was the presence of Wilbur and Orville Wright, along with their team of six pilots and planes.

Orville, in an aircraft launched from a monorail, was the first to take off. Walter Brookins, one of the Wright team pilots, broke the world altitude record that day when he rose to 4,384.5 feet.

Archrivals of Wright's fliers were the airmen of the Glenn Curtiss Exhibition Team. The two groups sometimes competed in the same air meets and, whether or not that was the case, always tried to exceed the performances of other pilots—flying faster, farther and higher. Crowds below expected them to provide greater and more dangerous stunts. The aircraft weren't as safe as the planes of today, of course. Pilots weren't in cockpits or cabins. They were out in the open, sitting on a wing. There were accidents, and flying was a very dangerous business.

Two of the most popular pilots during the first year of exhibitions were Ralph Johnstone and Archibald Hoxsey, known as "the heavenly twins" because of their continuous efforts to set altitude records. In August 1910, just two months after the exhibitions started, Johnstone was flying a Model B at Asbury Park, New Jersey, and smashed into parked cars while landing. A month after that, Hoxsey crashed into the Wisconsin State Fair grandstand at Milwaukee and injured ten people. On a happier note, he gave Teddy Roosevelt his first plane ride on October 11, 1910, during an aviation meet in St. Louis.

However, in the waning days of the year, a double dose of tragedy ended the lives of both Johnstone and Hoxsey. On November 17 at Denver, Johnstone went into a spiraling dive and never pulled out. His death was the first of an American aviator. Then, while trying to set a new altitude record at Los Angeles on December 31, Hoxsey perished in a dive almost identical to Johnstone's.

A LIFE-SAVING DISAPPOINTMENT?

Had it not been for Archibald Hoxsey's judgment when he arrived at the Wisconsin State Fair in the Milwaukee suburb of West Allis more than a century ago, I might never have met and married the girl of my dreams, Martha Debbink, forty years later.

At the time Hoxsey appeared at the fair, Martha's father, Henry Debbink, was an eighteen-year-old student at the University of Wisconsin. When he learned the aviator planned to take up a few passengers, he applied to be one of them. Soon, he received a response saying he had been approved to go up in the plane. The message advised him to bring along the letter, which had a handwritten note at the bottom: "Mr. Hoxsey: The bearer is entitled to have the privilege of going with you as a passenger on the airship."

However, when Hoxsey arrived and saw the fairgrounds, according to the *Milwaukee Sentinel*, he complained to fair officials that they had not "provided a proper place for me to start and land." He added, "At first, I was determined not to make any flights at all, but then, when I had told the board that they must assume responsibility, I decided to fly."

He did go up on Tuesday, Wednesday, Thursday and Friday—but he also had advised officials he would not take any passengers with him because he considered "the grounds exceedingly unfavorable for flight except under the best of conditions."

So Henry Debbink didn't get to fly. And, who knows, that may have saved his life!

Henry Debbink, who was scheduled to fly with Archibald Hoxsey at the Wisconsin State Fair in 1910, stands with his daughter, Martha, at her wedding forty years later.

Hoxsey's Friday flight had hardly gotten underway before it ended. As his plane lifted from the racetrack and passed the grandstand, a gust of wind lifted the left wing, turning the aircraft into the stands where it landed atop several people. The *Sentinel* reported that ten were injured; the *Milwaukee Journal* said the number was eight, then followed with nine names in a list of those with injuries.

Of course, an accident that serious—or worse—could have happened during any of the flights at the fair. So it may be fortunate for Mr. Debbink—and for me—that Hoxsey decided not to take passengers up in West Allis that week.

—Gordon G. Beld

That second death within six weeks dampened spirits of the Wrights, of course, and deepened the brothers' concern about whether the exhibitions should continue. Their sister, Katharine, was especially upset and said, "New Year's Day was a nightmare for all. I am so sick of this exhibition business. It is so absolutely wrong."

There were no further deaths to Wright fliers during the following months, but as 1911 wore on, Wilbur and Orville became increasingly convinced that exhibition flying was not only endangering pilots but also was not as profitable as they had hoped. In November of that year, they called a halt to the exhibitions. Most of the fliers, however, bought planes and continued on their own.

Turpin went west with his close friend Philip Parmelee, a Michigan native who was born in Matherton and then lived in Marion, St. Johns, Mancelona and Flint before joining the Wright team in 1910.

During the ten months from November 1910 through September 1911, Parmelee chalked up an amazing number of aviation firsts—first flight carrying air freight, bolts of silk from Dayton to Columbus, Ohio; first to instruct pilots for the U.S. Army Air Service; first to drop aerial bombs, a test at Selfridge Field in San Francisco; first air-to-ground military radio transmission, a message sent by his passenger, Lieutenant Paul Beck; first military reconnaissance from the air, a scouting mission along the Mexican border; and first parachute jump from an airplane, made from his plane by jumper Grant Martin at Venice Beach, California.

Memorial Day weekend in 1912 was a tragic one for the Wrights and their former exhibition pilots. Parmelee and Turpin were in the state of Washington, and on May 29, Turpin was flying at the Meadows Racetrack near Seattle. As he came in for a landing on the track in front of the grandstand, a photographer ran in front of the plane, and Turpin swerved to miss him. In doing so, he struck a pylon and pivoted into the grandstand, killing one person and injuring several others. Turpin himself was bruised and briefly unconscious.

Back in Dayton on the following day, the holiday, Wilbur Wright lost a battle with typhoid fever that had him bedridden for several weeks. His death left Orville lonely and depressed, but he continued the aviation business for another four years before selling it.

Wilbur's funeral was on June 1, and on that day in Washington, Parmelee was performing during an air show at a fairground near Yakima. He was in the air for only three minutes when a gust of wind hit the tail and flipped the plane. Parmelee hung on as he and the plane fell four hundred feet, crashing into a field three miles from the fairground. Farmers found his body under the engine and other debris. Before he took off, Parmelee was urged to postpone the flight, at least until the wind died down. But he merely laughed as he climbed into his seat.

Overwhelmed by the death of his friend, Turpin vowed never to fly again. He quickly went to Yakima to get Parmelee's body, then took it back to St. Johns, Michigan, for burial in Clinton County's East Plains Cemetery.

That wasn't the last tragic demise of a former Wright exhibition aviator. Just ten days after Parmelee's crash, there was another. This one was on the East Coast, where pilot Arthur L. Welsh was conducting ten required tests of an airplane being purchased by the Aeronautical Division of the U.S. Army Signal Corps. With him in the passenger seat as he took off from College Park, Maryland, on June 11, 1912, was Lieutenant Leighton W. Hazelhurst Jr., said to be one of the army's most promising young aviators.

The test to be performed involved a climb to two thousand feet within ten minutes while carrying a load of 450 pounds. Before attempting the climb, Welsh swooped past observing officers on the ground. As he did so, the plane's wings collapsed upward, their tips almost meeting above the engine. The aircraft dropped to earth, and both men died instantly. The bodies were taken by automobile to nearby Walter Reed Hospital, and within a few minutes of the takeoff, the flag at the field was at half-staff.

Three months later—September 15, 1912—at the Cicero Aviation Field near Chicago, the Wright biplane of Howard Gill collided with a monoplane flown by George Mestach. Gill, a former member of the Wright Exhibition Team, was killed when his plane fell two hundred feet and crashed. Mestach was injured but not seriously. The fliers were competing in the second annual International Aviation Meet of the Aero Club of Illinois. Ground-based planes flew from the Cicero airfield during the first four days of the meet and then action shifted to Grant Park at the lakefront for six days of hydroplane competition.

Gill was to compete with Tony Janus in a biplane race around a course marked by pylons in the day's final event. It was dusk and visibility was poor, so Gill told meet officials it was too dark to race and warned that there could be an accident if more than one plane would be in the air. But the fliers were ordered to proceed with the event. Some reports state officials forced the pilots to take off to avoid disappointing the crowd.

Mestach was scheduled to race against the clock in his monoplane, and he also protested against flying with inadequate visibility. He was assured by those running the meet that his plane would be the only one in the air. Gill and Janus had completed their race, but Gill had not yet landed when Mestach took off.

In the collision, the tail section of Gill's aircraft—with the rudder, elevator and stabilizer—was torn away. His death was the second at the meet. On the day before competition began, aviator Paul Peck was trying out a biplane he planned to use in the competition. He lost control, crashed and died soon after arriving at a hospital.

In concluding its account of the 1912 Gill-Mestach collision, the *New York Times* provided a chilling list of air tragedy statistics:

> *Gill is the ninth aviator to lose his life this month in a fall, and several have been badly injured. Two other accidents occurred this month in which five spectators were killed. The largest number of aviators to be killed in a single month is sixteen. Gill is the seventy-third airman to be killed this year. This equals the record year of 1911, when seventy-three were killed. The death of Gill yesterday brings the toll of those killed in aeroplane accidents since 1908, when aeroplane flying began on a large scale, up to 182.*

Fifteen years passed before another of the Wright Exhibition Team fliers perished. Leonard Bonney had a close call in 1914 when he performed above a fairground at Bellefonte, Pennsylvania. He had reached an altitude of 1,200 feet when a thin wire holding the elevator of his plane snapped. Fire broke out in the uncontrollable aircraft just before it crashed, but miraculously, Bonney survived. Had he been knocked unconscious, he would have perished. Flames destroyed the canvas wings and tail before the first would-be rescuer arrived.

During the rest of that decade, Bonney was involved with several military aviation activities—training pilots for the army at Roosevelt Field and the navy at Smith's Point, both on Long Island; flying with the first aerial anti-submarine patrol in an unsuccessful effort to find German sub U-53; and teaching Mexican government pilots the technique of dropping bombs.

During the 1920s, Bonney designed and developed an airplane that was a preview of World War II's gull-winged Chance Vought F4U Corsair. Fascinated by seagulls, he believed a gull-shaped plane would be better than most of those then in the air. His *Bonney Gull* was so gull-like that it looked as though the wings could flap. They couldn't, but they could fold in a way that would help brake the plane in landing—and in another way so that the aircraft would need less space for storage. With several features far ahead of their time, the *Bonney Gull* was an interesting and impressive machine.

After wind-tunnel and ground tests, the plane was ready for a flight test, and Bonney took off on May 4, 1928, from Roosevelt Field on Long Island, the airport from which Lindbergh zoomed into the sky on his historic flight across the Atlantic a year earlier. The *Bonney Gull* raced down the runway and rose smoothly into the air. But when it reached an altitude of only a hundred feet, the aircraft nosed over and dived to the ground. Bonney was killed instantly.

Bonney was the sixth, and last, of the Wright Exhibition Team members to die in a crash. Though many other pioneer pilots perished, Clifford Turpin—who had brought heavier-than-air flight to Grand Rapids and who refused to continue flying after Parmelee's death—lived to the age of seventy-nine.

CHAPTER 5

A Few Chills for a Newsman

After his flight in the Wright Model B plane at the West Michigan State Fair on September 12, 1911, newsman J.E. Worthington recounted in a page one story of the next day's edition of the Grand Rapids News *what he saw and how he felt—fearful, thrilled and amazed. Following are excerpts from his story, which filled 461 lines of type on pages one and ten of the paper.*

Aviator Turpin and I did a little flying yesterday at the West Michigan State Fair at Comstock Park and landed somewhat unexpectedly in a marsh. It was on the west side of the river above the hydraulic plant and in about the most inaccessible spot in Grand Rapids.

We splashed through marsh and bog in the machine, hurdled a two-foot ditch and came to a stop in a swale.

Three kids popped out of the grass like frogs.

"Hello, fellow, whadja come down for?" they inquired.

Mr. Turpin was very kind. He explained that the engine had stopped and that he had felt it necessary to come down, as it was impossible to stay up longer.

They desired to know what made it stop.

He did not know that himself just then, so we pressed them into service and began to haul the forty-foot biplane out of the mud.

It was a good deal of a job, for when we climbed out of the machine we stepped into water over our shoe tops. Other kids arrived in squads and finally by battalions. William Bergsma, 184 Dean Street, came along with a friend in a motor boat and we soon had the machine out of the mire.

Here are the seats where the pilot and passenger sat in early Wright planes. No wonder *Grand Rapids News* writer J.E. Worthington was a bit edgy! Just sitting out in the open on a wing offered virtually no protection. *Courtesy of Library of Congress.*

"Did it scare you?" seven thousand people have asked.

"Sure," is the correct answer.

Wouldn't it scare you? The machine was perhaps 400 or 500 feet in the air...

I never fell off a Lutheran church, but have heard it referred to as some drop, and this may have been like that.

At any rate, we dipped sharply and most speedily for perhaps fifty feet, and I was badly scared...

If I had known more about the machine, it would have been apparent that the engine was missing fire, but it did not occur to me.

We kept sliding to the earth, heading toward the west side of the stream, but I did not think of landing until we were fifty feet from the ground.

Turpin had been looking for a smooth spot to land. It struck me a soft spot would be better...

There is a strip of dry land perhaps one hundred feet wide between the stream and the marsh. We hit this and ran along at full speed for perhaps a hundred yards, hurdling a two-foot ditch, splashing mud and water and sedge in all directions and landing in a swale.

Then came the kids with their inquiries about our safety.

Turpin landed while laughing.

"How would you like to come down 3,000 feet that way?" he asked.

Frankly, the idea didn't seem reasonable. I told him so.

"Well, you've had an experience not one passenger in a thousand gets," he said.

Then we set in to pull the plane out of the mud. A great mass of mud and sedge was tangled about one of the wheels, and the bottom of the under plane *[lower wing]* was splashed with mud and water.

We hauled it back on level—or approximately level—ground and Turpin toyed with the engine.

Bergsma and his friend spun the propeller blades, and when everything seemed to be all right Turpin tried it again. The run was short and the ground very hummocky, so that he wouldn't try to take me up again.

His first try was a failure. The machine rose perhaps a hundred feet into the air. Turpin circled around for half a mile and came flying back for a landing at the same point. This time, however, he avoided the swale.

The people at the fairgrounds had seen the first rapid shoot downward; and Turpin's mechanician *[mechanic]*, Fred Caro, commandeering the first auto he could get, raced down Canal Street, thinking the plane was on the east side of the stream.

Bergsma ferried them across in his motor boat, and they went at the engine. Pretty soon Turpin, after fumbling about with a screwdriver and prying the lid off several matters, lifted out a piece of iron.

"Here you are, Mr. Motorboat Man," said he.

Bergsma looked it over and smiled. "I've had the same trouble," said he.

The spark plug in the second cylinder had become flooded with oil and burned out, throwing the cylinder out of commission. A new one was fitted in, and the aviator was off again for the fairgrounds. Circling once above the heads of the hundred or so people who had gathered, he went off like a shot for the fairgrounds.

Caro, the mechanician, and myself ferried ourselves over the swamp to the road that runs along the railroad tracks and took an automobile to the fairgrounds. The trip was over.

At this point in his story, Worthington goes back to the beginning of the flight and describes the field from which Turpin and he took off and why they flew from there rather than the fairgrounds.

The start, carrying double, was made from Irve Woodworth's back forty. Turpin found it the first time up in the afternoon. He did not like to risk taking up a passenger from the infield at the fairgrounds, fearing that perhaps he might not make height quickly enough to avoid telegraph wires or buildings. In consequence he went scouting about for a better field to take on passengers and found it. The crowd generally did not know of the arrangement and, when he started alone on the second trip, thought no passenger was to be taken…

Wheeling the machine to the west side of the field, it was turned about so as to start toward the northeast, from which direction what little breeze there was seemed to be blowing.

Crawling into the machine, no little feat when one is not accustomed to the tangle of wire and frames which must be passed, the two of us sat down while he gave me the final instructions. The seat is the size of a circus reserved seat.

"You can hang on to this wire or this brace if you feel the need of something to hold to," said he.

The wire was one of two directly in front of us and presses against the breast of passenger and aviator. The brace was the big one that rises directly in front of the engine.

"Don't touch this lever," he continued, "and on no account touch this wire. That stops the engine which is a highly undesirable thing to happen."

The lever was a companion piece to the one he handled, raising or lowering the planes [wings]…The wire is a loose one that passed directly above our heads in front and swung around on a little pulley in the engine. I wouldn't have laid hands on either one of them for a four-dollar bill.

Then Turpin gave the word to Young [another mechanic]. A whirl of the blades, a clatter as of forty motor boats, and we set off across the level field.

It didn't seem nearly so level. We hit every bump, and when you are going twenty or twenty-five miles an hour in a light machine like a biplane there are an awful lot of bumps to hit…For a few minutes while the trip lasted, I thought the machine might go to pieces and spill us out before we left the ground.

Then, before I knew it, we were in the air. Turpin had given the plane a little upward twitch and we leaped away from the ground as easily as if flying had been an age old art. The chief sensation was before the bumping stopped. Before I realized that we had started from the ground, we were ten feet in the air and—GOING UP…

Fearing dizziness, I did not look directly down for some time, but kept my attention fixed on the points farther toward the horizon and watched the vast and beautiful view unfold.

It is a glorious county, this of Kent, and absolutely the best way to see it is from above. All the imperfections are ironed out and the whole countryside looks like a park, with the little fields laid off in regular blocks and the intersecting roads cutting them at intervals.

Swinging gradually from the northeast to the southwest, we headed over toward the fairgrounds…The view over the rifle range was superb. By this time we had swung about enough so that the fair buildings began to loom up…

Trees looked like saplings, and the undergrowth was more like weeds than small trees. We could see boats on the river. As we passed over the river directly in front of the tannery, I looked down and could see very plainly the wide ribbon of refuse the big plant throws into the stream. There is a strip forty feet wide or more that looks like cold tea from above. One could almost imagine, on looking into the clearer water, that he could see the bottom of the stream.

Then we sailed over the fairgrounds…The chief impression was that the grounds were very untidy. The crowds had pressed to the race course to see the machine pass over. The waste paper that they had spread in two days showed up very plainly. The ground was almost covered with it. The tents looked small and the buildings were very flat from above.

"How do you like it?" Turpin shouted in my ear.

I could guess, rather than hear, what he said, for the clatter of the engine was terrific.

"Fine!" I shouted back. "It's great!"

So it was. There was no sensation of unsteadiness. Dizziness did not bother me, and there was nothing to detract from the fun.

There was little or no impression of speed, though we were going forty-five miles an hour…The horizon comes up to meet you, but it is not close by as the trees are outside of a railroad train window. The wind blows stiffly in your face, but there is nothing else to indicate that there is any great speed.

Conversation is impossible. If any great thoughts surge in you, there is nothing to do but throw out a life line to them and utter them when you get down. And, if you come down in a hurry, you are apt to forget all the great thoughts. I did.

Which brings me pretty near to the end of my yarn. A newspaperman may criticize an aviator for the imperfect terminal facilities—and I must say that there is still much to be desired in that way—but he must have some of his own, or he is subject for criticism, too.

So, merely remarking that the term "bird man" and the term "hangar" have not been used in this story, I draw it to a close.

CHAPTER 6

Barnstormer, Bootlegger and Battler for Survival

Soon after heavier-than-air craft appeared in the sky, barnstorming pilots began touring the country to demonstrate aerial maneuvers and take passengers aloft for views that only birds and balloonists had seen before. Some came individually, others in groups known as flying circuses, and persuaded farmers to let them operate from one of their fields.

One of the first of these to make a stop in Grand Rapids was Bert R.J. Hassell. It was in 1914 that he came to the city in a Curtiss biplane and thrilled crowds with his stunt flying, then took some of the more daring spectators up for an even more exciting experience.

There were plenty of crashes in those days, and Hassell had his share. One resulted in the nickname by which he was better known for the rest of his life. In early 1915, he learned of a good deal on a flying boat owned by Harold McCormick, chairman of International Harvester, and went to Lake Forest, Illinois, to check it out. Frosty March winds were whipping up waves on Lake Michigan, but he took the plane up for a trial. Then, to impress those on the shore with his flying skill, he leveled off just four or five feet above the water. A large wave hit the tail section, and the plane plunged into the lake at ninety miles an hour.

Hassell had a rudder wire twisted around one of his legs but managed to free himself and started to swim toward shore. "Swimming in Lake Michigan in March is like a dip in liquid ice," he said later. McCormick's gardener paddled a canoe out to Hassell, who grabbed an edge of the craft and was towed to shore. Someone in the crowd of spectators shouted, "Anyone who

Bert "Fish" Hassell and an unidentified young lady (at right) pause alongside his flying boat at Lake Muskegon with Tony Stadlman and his wife, Gertrude. Hassell bought the aircraft from Illinois industrialist Harold McCormick and used it during the summer of 1915 to take passengers up for exciting views of the Lake Michigan shoreline. *Courtesy of Midway Village Museum, Rockford, Illinois.*

can swim in that water must be a fish." From then on, Hassell had a new nickname—"Fish."

He bought the seaplane and used it that summer to taxi commuters from Chicago suburbs to the Loop.

Two years later, Hassell was back for a longer stay in West Michigan. During the summer of 1916, the flying boat he had purchased from McCormick was used to take passengers up for thrilling views of the Lake Michigan shoreline near Muskegon. The plane then was based at Muskegon Lake.

Then Grand Rapids businessmen Fred Pantlind and Jewell Clark recruited him to assist in the development of a flying school they planned to develop at the shore of Reeds Lake in East Grand Rapids. He and two other pilots, Tony Stadlman and P.G.B. "Bud" Morriss, were ground-school and flight instructors; and the three began rebuilding a Benoist flying boat that Morriss had purchased. Work began in a nearby garage and then was moved to a hangar at the edge of the lake. Bert Kenyon, of Grand Rapids, who had been taught to fly by Hassell, rebuilt the engine of the plane.

When it was ready to fly, Kenyon and Hassell slid the hydroplane down a ramp and into the lake for a test flight. "I was at the controls," Hassell recalled, "and Kenyon was standing beside the engine to adjust the two carburetors...We began to gather speed, and I thought we were about to become airborne when a cylinder suddenly broke loose. Then a piston went through the engine head. I chopped the throttle and cut the switch quickly, but Kenyon and I nevertheless got a hot-water shower from the radiator coolant."

By the time the engine was repaired, local enthusiasm about aviation had cooled and the flying school began to lose students. After the engine was reinstalled, Hassell soared over Grand Rapids for a half hour "to demonstrate we had an airplane that would really fly." But the flying school idea was dead.

With World War I raging abroad as the prospects for success at Reeds Lake faded, Hassell and others from the group decided to try producing flying boats for the U.S. Army and Navy. That venture, known as Michigan Aviation Company, was based in a building that now is the Wealthy Theater. It, too, did not last long.

Hassell then joined the Fourth Aero Squadron as a civilian flight instructor in Illinois. However, with the fighting of World War I continuing, he quit that $700-a-month job and enlisted in the army as a private, earning $30 a month. Eventually, he became a lieutenant and continued as an instructor through the years of World War I.

In 1919, he was back in Grand Rapids as chief pilot for Roseswift Airplane Company. His job was flying passengers and freight between Grand Rapids and Ionia, as well as offering weekend airplane rides at Grand Rapids and nearby small towns. When Roseswift folded a year later, Hassell delivered suits by plane from a Chicago clothier to customers within a fifty-mile radius.

After that, he flew airmail and then joined the staff of the Lincoln School of Aviation in Nebraska. A school in name only, it gave exhibitions and rides at fairgrounds and occasionally made charter flights. But this was the Prohibition era, and the real moneymaker for the business was transporting bootlegged booze in from Canada. When lawmen began moving in, Hassell went to the East Coast and flew a six-passenger flying boat converted for use as a firewater ferry. The illicit freight was picked up from ships on the ocean and flown to shore. When that operation also became risky, he returned to Chicago and flew whiskey from Ontario to a Wabash Avenue speakeasy.

Fish's fellow fliers at the Reeds Lake and Michigan Aviation hydroplane projects also moved on to interesting, though less bizarre, experiences.

Stadlman teamed up with Allan Lockheed in an exhibition flying venture and then in the formation of what became the Lockheed Aircraft Company. He was superintendent of the Lockheed factory at Santa Barbara at the time the company developed its Vega, subsequent versions of which were flown by Amelia Earhart and Wiley Post. The six-passenger monoplane was used by Earhart when she became the first woman to fly the Atlantic, and Post twice flew around the world in the *Winnie Mae*, a white Vega with purple trim.

Before his days in Grand Rapids, Morris was the first to develop wireless communication while in flight, using the Marconi system; operated a flying boat service on the lake front in Chicago; was managing editor of an aviation weekly, *Aero & Hydro*; opened the Bud Morriss Flying School; and was vice-president and engineer of Benoist Airplane Company at St. Louis.

After the project at Reeds Lake, he enlisted in the navy and served for a year and a half during World War I, then was executive officer at a naval aviation school. In the late 1920s, several pioneer pilots decided to form an association whose members had made solo flights before America's entry into World War I. Morris was elected the first president of the group known as the Early Birds Society. He also became involved in broadcasting and hotel management.

Kenyon is the only member of the Reeds Lake crew who remained in Grand Rapids. Besides his experience with hydroplanes, he was interested in land planes and obtained permission from the Kent County Board of Supervisors for planes to take off and land at the old fairgrounds, which later became the first Kent County Airport. In 1925, he and Russell Shaw designed and constructed the first administration building at the airport.

He left the city for a time during World War I to supervise installation of dual controls, which he had invented, on army planes at McCook Field at Dayton, Ohio. His device enabled instructors to disengage the controls used by their students. He also supervised a school in Grand Rapids to teach Great Lakes Naval Training Station personnel techniques for aircraft assembly and motor work.

In 1916, Kenyon and a friend brought joy to many Grand Rapids children when they parachuted hundreds of toys over the city. The venture was sponsored by a local department store, and the store manager arranged for them to drop a large banner, which could be read as it fell to the ground. It landed atop a tree in the manager's yard where it hung for days, readable to all who passed. When the manager called to remark on the amazing accuracy of the bombardment, Kenyon responded, "When we do a job, we do it right!"

In 1926, Kenyon became traffic manager for the first passenger airline in America, Detroit-Grand Rapids Airline, which was affiliated with Stout Air Service. The line began operations with the "Tin Goose" planes, which were powered by a four-cycle engine. Later, Ford Trimotors replaced them.

When Charles Lindbergh visited Grand Rapids after his history-making flight across the Atlantic in 1927, Kenyon took care of his plane, the *Spirit of St. Louis*, during his stay. Later in life, he operated a taxicab company in Grand Rapids and was owner of a bowling alley, Pla-Mor Lanes on South Division Avenue.

"Fish" Hassell's exciting adventures continued for a lifetime. During the 1920s, he dreamed of pioneering a commercial air route over the Arctic between North America and Europe, the one now most used to link the two continents. While a reserve officer in the U.S. Army Air Corps in 1923, he wrote a report on the pros and cons of flying across the Arctic.

In the late 1920s, he decided he'd fly from his hometown of Rockford, Illinois, to Sweden, the homeland of his ancestors. He took a bus to the Stinson Aircraft Company in Northville, Michigan, and arranged to have his friend, Eddie Stinson, build a plane to his specifications. Before returning to Illinois, he contacted Professor William Hobbs of the University of Michigan, who was planning a 1928 expedition to Greenland. Hassell asked him to clear a landing strip and make arrangements for refueling at his base of operations.

On July 26, 1928, Hassell and his copilot, Parker "Shorty" Cramer, took off in their plane, a Stinson Detroiter named the *Greater Rockford*. But moments later it crashed in a cornfield. The plane was repaired, and they tried again on August 16. After a refueling stop at Cochrane, Ontario, they headed for Greenland. As they neared Hobbs's base, however, they ran into adverse weather and their fuel gauge read empty. Unable to locate the landing strip, Hassell put the plane down on the ice cap. His landing was perfect, but their situation was perilous. Far from their target, they had no gloves and their only food supply was ten pounds of pemmican.

They started out on foot, expecting to reach Hobbs's base in a couple days and return to the plane with fuel. For six days, they struggled through mountains and across icy rivers wearing wet clothes that never dried. Then they reached the tundra, and Cramer fell into quicksand. Hassell rescued him by extending a rifle that, fortunately, he was carrying. Then they encountered swarms of mosquitoes.

After two weeks, Hobbs was sure the fliers had perished. When two Eskimos reported seeing smoke, however, two members of the expeditionary

With his plane, the *Greater Rockford*, Bert "Fish" Hassell attempted to prove in 1928 that an air route across the Arctic to Europe would be better than the one Lindbergh flew a year earlier. He and copilot Parker "Shorty" Cramer took off from Rockford, Illinois, and headed for Sweden. However, they were forced to land on the ice cap in Greenland and trudged through snow and mountains for two weeks before being rescued. *Courtesy of Midway Village Museum, Rockford, Illinois.*

The frigid and rugged terrain of Greenland looks the same from the air in this 2012 view as it did to "Fish" Hassell and copilot "Shorty" Cramer just before their fuel was exhausted and they were forced to land on the ice cap in 1928. *Courtesy of Antxon Basurko.*

crew set out across the fjord in a small boat with an outboard motor, found Hassell and Cramer and brought them to their camp.

On September 3, the fliers left with Hobbs and his crew aboard the sloop *Nakuak* and headed for Greenland's capital. Near the midpoint of the trip, the boat struck a reef. The personnel and equipment were evacuated safely, but the *Nakuak* sank. Eventually, the pilots made it back to New York, where they were welcomed with a ticker-tape parade. From there, they went to the nation's capital, where Hassell met President Calvin Coolidge and future president Herbert Hoover during a visit to the White House.

Soon after his return, Hassell worked as a salesman for Stinson. But he became discouraged when the company merged with Cord Corporation after the 1929 stock market crash. Then Eddie Stinson was killed in a plane crash at Chicago in 1932, and Hassell left the company. He was employed briefly by a Cleveland airplane manufacturer before going back to Illinois, where he made and sold ice cream bars and popcorn.

However, he couldn't stay out of the air, and in 1935, he returned to aviation with the Bellanca Aircraft Corporation in Delaware. A few years later, he came back to Illinois and sold airplane fasteners made by the Rockford Screw Products Company. His first order—which totaled $750,000—was for fasteners used in the manufacture of B-24 Liberator bombers at Willow Run, Michigan.

In January 1942, just weeks after the Japanese attacked Pearl Harbor and plunged the United States into World War II, Hassell was called back to active duty in the army as a colonel. He first was ordered to establish a base in Greenland and then was appointed commanding officer of the Air Transport Command Base at Goose Bay, Labrador.

He was surprised one day in 1944 when the crew of an army survey plane came to his office with a photograph they had taken of an old airplane lying upside down on the ice in Greenland. The tail had been torn off, apparently by the same winds that had overturned the aircraft. It was Hassell's *Greater Rockford*. War correspondent Bob Considine asked Hassell for a copy of the picture to use with a report he was writing on the commander and the Goose Bay operation. "Hell, no!" was the reply. "You think I want to have one of those lugs I used to fly with say that Fish landed the ship on its back?"

After the war, Hassell went to Iceland for American Airlines as a vice-president in charge of Meeks Field, where planes were refueled during the Berlin Airlift. Then, in 1950, when the Korean War broke out, he was involved with the Flying Tigers Line in supplying United Nations troops. That ended when he was called back to active duty in the air force to build a base at Thule, Greenland, on the route that Soviet bombers would have had to use to reach the United States. His next assignment was construction of a base in northern Norway. His final air force job was reactivation of bases in England. That ended when he turned sixty and had to retire from military service.

In 1955, the Foundation Company of Canada persuaded Hassell to serve as assistant project manager for construction of the Distant Early Warning (DEW) Line, a system of radar stations for detection of Soviet bombers during the Cold War. By then, doctors had given him only two years to live because of prostate cancer, but he spent more than two years on the project before leaving the Arctic for the last time.

Aviation artist Robert Catlin, also a native of Rockford, suggested to Hassell in the late 1960s that they try to recover the *Greater Rockford*, which had been encased in Greenland ice for four decades. Catlin led an effort to get support for the venture, and Hassell's son Vic took part in the recovery effort. He called his father in September 1968 to report that the old Stinson was awaiting shipment to the United States. On June 17, 1969, a C-46 transport landed at the airfield in Rockford with the old plane aboard.

It was donated to the SST Aviation Exhibit Center at Kissimmee, Florida, which agreed to rebuild the aircraft. But no effort was made in that direction, so Hassell decided it should come back to Illinois and become part of a new museum complex that opened at Rockford in 1974. However, he died on September 12 of that year without that taking place. In 1975, however, a local department store offered to bring the plane back as its contribution to Rockford's celebration of the bicentennial. Today, the *Greater Rockford*, looking just like it did when it took off nearly a century ago, is on display at Midway Village Museum in Rockford, Illinois.

CHAPTER 7

Flying at the Fair

A s the twentieth century dawned, the Wright Brothers were still flying gliders and their historic powered flight at Kitty Hawk was still a few years away. So it's not likely that many in Grand Rapids at that time were thinking about the possibility of traveling through the sky. Most in West Michigan then were concerned that their biggest thrills, during one special week in autumn at least, were going to disappear.

For six straight years, 1895 through 1900, the Michigan State Fair had taken place at the new fairgrounds in Mill Creek just north of the city. Before that, the fair's location frequently changed, and the event was held at cities throughout the state. And now it was going to move again, this time to the east side of Michigan.

The ninety-acre fairground at Mill Creek had been donated by Charles C. Comstock, a former Grand Rapids mayor and congressman, just before the 1895 fair; and today the community near the site is known as Comstock Park.

Comstock's 1885–87 term as congressman from Michigan's fifth district immediately preceded that of the first Congressman Ford from Grand Rapids, Melbourne H. The second Congressman Ford from the fifth district was Gerald R., later vice president and president of the United States.

After Michigan determined the 1901 state fair would be in the Detroit area, folks at Grand Rapids decided they'd have their own state fair; and a year later the West Michigan State Fair was born. There was even aerial entertainment at that first state fair on the west side of the state—but not involving a balloon, dirigible or plane. This one was a group of fliers on trapeze bars.

Within a few years, however, aircraft began soaring through the sky above the fairgrounds; and these aeronautical exhibitions were the biggest attractions as far as most fairgoers were concerned.

Roy Knabenshue came with his dirigible in September 1907 and, according to the *Grand Rapids Herald*, shared the spotlight with "Spellman and his clever little bears." When they weren't performing, both the airship and the animals were kept in tents at the racetrack infield.

Fair officials hoped Knabenshue's dirigible would be able to carry passengers, but his aircraft that could have done that was destroyed in August when wind blew it into electric wires at the Iowa State Fair.

There apparently was a heavier-than-air machine at the fair in Des Moines that year, too. Amelia Earhart, who was then ten years old, later said that's where she saw an airplane for the first time. But it wasn't until years later that flying machines fascinated her. "It was a thing of rusty wire and wood," she said later, "and not at all interesting."

Knabenshue was able to bring another dirigible to the West Michigan fair, but that one was not capable of carrying passengers. After flying about the area during one of his flights, he circled the racetrack at the fairgrounds before landing. His time for the circuit was two minutes and forty-four seconds, according to bear-keeper Spellman.

Knabenshue was back at Comstock Park in 1909, this time with Lincoln Beachey, who then was still flying dirigibles. At the 1910 Los Angeles International Aviation Meet, he and his older brother, Hillery, were both competitors. Hillery flew a heavier-than-air machine while Lincoln's aircraft was a dirigible. After that meet, Lincoln never flew a dirigible again but became a spectacular and daring airplane pilot.

His flying career was cut short at the Panama-Pacific International Exposition at San Francisco in 1915 during the first exhibition of a monoplane in inverted flight. With 50,000 spectators at the fairgrounds and another 200,000 on nearby hills, he roared past and turned the plane on its back. When he attempted to pull the plane out of its inverted position, however, wing spars broke and the plane plunged into the bay. He survived the crash but died from drowning.

At Grand Rapids in 1909, he had narrowly averted disaster. According to the *Herald*'s report, "Beachey's car [dirigible] became entangled in the telegraph wires over the railroad track and, as it hung there, a train passed and the aviator was deluged with soot and smoke...The incident gave the crowd a nice thrill."

As noted previously, the first heavier-than-air machine to fly at Grand Rapids, with J. Clifford Turpin at the controls, was the main attraction of

Roy Knabenshue ascends from the fairground in his dirigible at the 1907 West Michigan State Fair. A few years later, he recruited the first pilots for Orville and Wilbur Wright's Exhibition Team.

After flying dirigibles for several years, Lincoln Beachey became one of the best of pioneer airplane pilots. However, at San Francisco in 1915, while performing the first exhibition of a monoplane in inverted flight, his aircraft plunged into the bay and he drowned. *Courtesy of Library of Congress.*

the 1911 West Michigan State Fair. Two years later, Hillery Beachey, a friend of Turpin, was the fair's star attraction. His performance, with companion fliers, was called "Battle of the Clouds," but on the first day it was to be staged, the sky battle was preceded by one on the ground. Many of those who had come to see the aerial conflict believed it was to be a free event, but that wasn't the case.

The next day's *Grand Rapids Press* described what happened:

> *The crowds surged about the grandstand demanding admittance, but hesitated when the admission price was added. Finally, boys began climbing over the lower sides of the grandstand. Services of several deputies were required to drive the crowd back. The deputies, distracted by a multitude of duties, could not control the crowd which increased with constant rapidity. Men and boys climbed fences and congregated in the race course in front of the grandstand and beyond the fence surrounding the track. Crowds pressed hard on either side of the grandstand, and women and girls stood on chairs to get a view of the place where the battle was to be presented.*

Beachey's agents told deputies there would be no exhibition until those in the crowd were driven back and made to pay. Sheriff's officers realized that, with only twenty-five deputies on hand, nothing short of calling out the militia could bring that about. Finally, the president of the fair association ordered that the show take place without charging those who had invaded the site. Additional deputies were hired to prevent a repetition of the problem during following days of the fair.

After the outbreak of World War I, the first conflict in which aircraft were used on a large scale, staged aerial battles on the homefront were sure to attract crowds. That happened at the West Michigan State Fair in 1915 when aviators John Hector Worden, Frank Champion and Louis Gertson staged the "Siege of Liege."

Worden, a Cherokee Native American, had military aviation experience. In 1912, during the early days of the Revolution in Mexico, he showed Mexican government forces how airplanes could be useful in their operations. He was persuaded to stay on and fly reconnaissance missions and was given the honorary rank of captain in the federal army. After he came back to the United States and wrote about his experiences, other aviators flocked to Mexico to fly for either government or rebel forces.

Champion was a photographer for the *Los Angeles Examiner* in 1910 when he covered the Dominguez Field Aviation meet and fell in love with aeronautics. Early the next year, he went to London and studied aviation at Hendon Aerodrome, then returned to the United States and obtained his pilot's license. In 1917, he went to Asia with the Katherine Stinson Flying Circus, and then extended his stay to establish a school for training Japanese pilots.

On October 30, Champion was flying at four thousand feet over the city of Kochi, and as he began maneuvering the plane, the left wing gave way and he plunged to earth. As the body was carried to a crematory, the procession passed through streets lined with thousands of Japanese, some in tears.

At the time Champion was in Japan, Gertson was flying exhibitions at fairs in the Midwest. At the Iowa State Fair in 1917, he flew at night with lights on the plane delineating his turns and loops. He performed at the fair again a year later, making two flights a day, one in the afternoon and another at night.

At Comstock Park in 1915, the trio amazed fair visitors with an array of stunts during early afternoon flights and then put on their battle simulation as evening approached. In its report of one of the performances, the *Herald* said:

> *Captain Worden in his monoplane hovered over the fortress of Liege, off in the race course enclosure, from behind which bombs were thrown at the aviator. Now and then he dropped one from his machine which was exploded in the air too high to endanger the lives of the men in the fortification. Meanwhile, Gertson in his biplane and Champion in a monoplane did scout work and flew high and at some distance away, looking for the air enemy who might be in the distance.*

As if the daring stunts of barnstormers weren't enough, wing-walking came to the West Michigan State Fair in 1919; and the hair-raising thrills probably prompted many in the crowd to turn their heads or close their eyes while Ormer Locklear stood on the wing of a plane as he and pilot Milton "Skeets" Elliott roared over the race track.

Locklear was a pilot in the U.S. Army Air Corps in 1917 when he began leaving the cockpits of planes so as to better see communications being signaled from the ground or to repair minor problems of the aircraft. After his military service, he thrilled crowds at county fairs as he walked on wings, clung from landing gears and rope ladders and transferred from one plane to another in midair.

At the 1919 fair in Comstock Park, Locklear and Elliott performed with another pilot, Shirley Short, and amazed spectators. The *Herald* said:

Wing-walker Ormer Locklear (center) and pilots Milton "Skeets" Elliott (right) and Shirley Short thrilled crowds at the 1919 West Michigan State Fair. A year later, Locklear and Elliott were killed when their plane failed to pull out of a dive while shooting the Hollywood film *Skywayman. Courtesy of Library of Congress.*

Never in all the history of spectacular activities in the Furniture City has there been anything that approached the feature offering at the West Michigan State Fair this year where Lieut. Ormer Locklear and his flying circus held the spectators on the fairgrounds spellbound by their daring acrobatics. Locklear with his thrilling change of planes in midair and his hair-raising stunts on the wings, the nose, the tail, and the undercarriage of a machine in full flight literally defies description.

Nevertheless, the paper did take a stab at describing:

First the lieutenant crept out on the lower wing, dropped down, slipped over the front edge, grasped the wing skid and let himself down. Hanging this way while pilot Short kept the ship on an even keel, they swept low over the grandstand. In a jiffy, Locklear was back in his seat. Next he appeared on the top wing, walked first to one end and then the other, stood upright on the pitching ship with hands extended over his head, and was nearly tossed into space by an air pocket. A moment later the crowd gasped when the plane circled and came back again with the lieutenant standing on his head in the middle of the top wing, his legs only inches from the flashing blades of the propeller.

Then came the climax:

> *He [Elliott] circled lazily over the field with motor at about three-quarters throttle while his chief was doing his stunts on Short's machine. Then at some signal Elliott dropped a rope ladder and they began to maneuver for the change. Locklear appeared on the top wing, walked out to the extreme left and stood there as the plane came back toward the stand on a northeasterly course over the track. They timed it just right. Elliott at greater altitude and farther back, dipped down, gaining on Short's machine with Locklear balanced precariously on the tip of the wing. Right over the center of the infield the top plane came down to within six feet of Locklear. It was over in a flash. Locklear had the rope ladder. Elliott zoomed up with him while Short went into a nose dive to be sure and clear everything. With Locklear hanging on the ladder, Elliott circled the field several times and then, with the daring acrobat safe in his seat, Elliott put the ship into a vertical bank, less than 300 feet in the air, and every aviator in the crowd involuntarily cried in protest. But Elliott straightened her out just above the track, roared past the stand, took his aerial bow and was gone.*

By the time of the 1919 fair, Locklear had become a star performer in sensational Hollywood productions; and less than a year later, he had a lead role in Fox Film Corporation's *The Skywayman*. The script called for a final aerial stunt of diving over oil fields at night with phosphorous flares blazing on the wings to make it appear the plane was afire. Elliott was pilot of the plane, which was illuminated by searchlights during the night of the flight in August 1920.

So that he'd know when to pull out of his dive, the director of the film was asked to turn off the lights when the plane reached a certain level. But he failed to do so, and by the time Elliott and Locklear knew how close they were to the ground, pulling out of the dive was impossible. The crash killed them both. The tragedy was good publicity for the film, Fox believed, and the footage was rushed into production. Even the final fatal plunge was screened.

Another wing-walker, this one a woman, was the headliner at the fair in 1921. That's when Ruth Law brought her three-plane flying circus and performed with male aeronautic experts Louis James and Verne Treat. In

Aviatrix and wing-walker Ruth Law was the main attraction at the Comstock Park fairground in 1921. The other stars of her flying circus were seventeen-year-old wing-walker Louis James and pilot Verne Treat. *Courtesy of Library of Congress.*

its account of their exhibitions, the *Grand Rapids Press* described Law as "the daring aviatrix whose stunts atop a swiftly flying airplane are thrilling thousands all this week at the West Michigan State Fair."

The three presented a show each evening with Law standing on the wing of a plane as it did loop-the-loops and figure eights and James transferring from a racing automobile to a plane piloted by Treat.

Law began flying in 1912 and was the first woman to loop-the-loop and the first to fly at night. During World War I, she went to the White House and asked President Woodrow Wilson for permission to fly with American forces in Europe. Her request was denied, but she did have authority to wear a uniform and she flew exhibitions for Liberty Loan and Red Cross fund drives.

She continued flying in barnstorming exhibitions for a few years after the war, until one day in 1922, when she picked up a newspaper and read a report saying she was retiring. Her husband, Charles Oliver, decided to end his worry about her life-threatening activities. He made the announcement without telling her, but she took it well. "I've been in the limelight long enough," she said. "I'm going to let him run things hereafter."

James, just seventeen years old, was said to be the youngest wing walker in the country. When he asked Law for a job doing aerial stunts, she tried to discourage him by telling him he'd need to walk on a wing the first time he went up. But she gave him a chance after he explained he had learned how to perform stunts in the loft of his father's barn.

A year after his appearance in Grand Rapids, he was killed while attempting to transfer from one plane to another at Chicago. An International News Service report said, "The rope ladder, from which he hung suspended from one plane, swung his body directly into the propeller of the other plane. His body was cut to pieces and fell mangled, almost at the foot of his sweetheart who was watching his performance."

Treat left the barnstorming business a few years later and flew airmail deliveries for Eastern Air Lines. But that was hardly less dangerous than exhibition flying. This was pointed out in a 1936 story by Scripps-Howard Newspapers staff writer Ernie Pyle who later, as a Pulitzer Prize–winning correspondent, told the stories of American fighting men in Europe and the Pacific during World War II.

Pyle's feature told how Treat twice during airmail flights had to jump for his life and twenty times wrecked planes in forced landings at night. "That sounds as if he wasn't a good pilot," Pyle wrote. "But it wasn't his fault the engines quit, and it takes superb skill to land just any old place and not kill yourself. Treat never had a scratch."

The story also told of a snowy night near Washington, D.C., when Treat had to jump from his plane. He was unaware that he was only three hundred feet up, and his chute opened just as he hit the ground. On another occasion, he ran out of gas and had to land. He dropped a flare, which set grass afire, and that prompted reports all over the country that he had crashed in flames and burned to death.

But Treat retired from flying in 1932 and went into the more peaceful business of selling automobiles at his dealership in Freehold, New Jersey. That's where Pyle found him and interviewed him. Early in his story, he wrote, "I came past Freehold today to see Treat for the first time since he quit flying. We were old friends and I wanted to say hello. I also wanted to see if a man can really get flying out of his blood. I still don't know."

And he concluded, "We talked for another hour, I guess, and Verne said: 'I'm sure glad you came past, and I'm not kiddin' either.' He looked younger and gayer than I had ever seen him, but I don't know yet whether that is because he stopped flying, or started thinking about it again."

CHAPTER 8

A Flying Field and a National First

The year was 1919—less than a decade after the first airplane appeared in the sky above Grand Rapids. Several local men had learned to fly, formed the Aero Club of Grand Rapids and were taking off and landing, usually from farmers' fields at the edge of the city. What needed to happen, they believed, was for an airport to be established in the metropolitan area.

By this time, government officials realized that the fascinating new flying machines could carry passengers and freight from one city to another. If that were to happen, Grand Rapids would need to keep pace—and that, too, would require a suitable landing field.

Mayor Christian Gallmeyer wanted to be sure the best site for such a facility would be selected, so he appointed businessman John Thomas Batts as chairman of a committee that would consider possibilities and make a recommendation.

The *Grand Rapids Herald* reported the group's findings in its Sunday edition on June 29, 1919:

> *Chairman Batts and a committee of reserve aviators last week inspected a number of possible sites, with the result that the Reeds Lake landing field for land and water planes has been recommended to the city fathers as best suited for the city's needs.*
>
> *The result of their findings has progressed into tentative plans for a permanent aerial station. The hangars are to be so constructed that the building may be first created with only one hangar and then gradually*

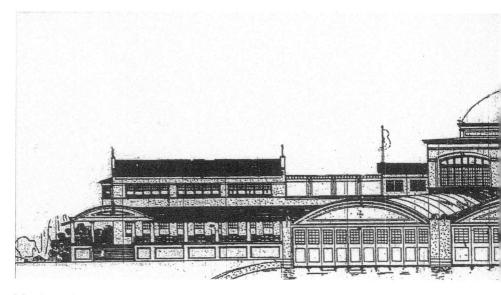

Members of a committee charged with finding the best site for a Grand Rapids airport in 1919 recommended that it be on the shore of Reeds Lake in East Grand Rapids. This architect's sketch shows the building they hoped would be erected at the edge of the lake. Its hangars and other facilities would accommodate hydroplanes on one side and land planes on the other.

added onto until the combined structure, embracing club rooms, land and water hangars, work shops, offices, dancing pavilion, and flyers' quarters are completed and the permanent station equipped to accommodate both government, commercial, and sport aviators and their planes.

Specifications call for spacious club rooms to be occupied by the Grand Rapids Aero Club. Repair shops, workshops, and library reading rooms, bedrooms and offices of the club are designed so as to assure a modern, up-to-the-minute station.

Above the story, an architect's sketch of the proposed facility stretched across all seven columns of the newspaper page. The committee suggested that the building should be erected at the shore of Reeds Lake so that it could be used by both land-based aircraft and hydroplanes. It would be an impressive structure, for sure. But it was never built.

Four months later—on October 29—the Kent County Board of Supervisors approved the Aero Club's request to use 120 acres of county-owned property in Paris Township as a landing field. For several years, this

parcel of land at the south edge of the Madison Avenue and Thirty-second Street intersection had been a fairground that attracted huge crowds—at least for a few autumn days when farmers displayed crops and livestock while fun-seekers found thrills on the midway.

That had ended, and in 1916, the county acquired the property and used it as a farm where prisoners raised crops. Then some of the early local fliers began to use it for takeoffs and landings. And now this would become the area's first airport—one that would serve as the center of Grand Rapids area aviation activities for nearly a half century.

Bert Kenyon, pioneer aviator who was involved in a flying boat project at Reeds Lake, had become interested in land-based planes and made the initial request to the county board. Someone would be needed to supervise activities at the field, of course, and Kenyon, in an interview with a *Herald* writer many years later, said he was given the job and became the first manager of what eventually would become Kent County Airport.

At the beginning, the Aero Club was given a five-year lease at no charge; but any improvements made were to be at the club's expense.

Another stimulus for development of the field was establishment of the city's first airline. Arthur Rosenthal—the would-be pilot of the Bissell-Mason plane that failed to get into the air in 1910—joined Tom Swift to form the Roseswift Airplane Company in 1919. Others involved in the effort were B.D. Coats, Fred Kramer and Harry Shields.

The *Grand Rapids Press* reported that the group began operations with a single Canadian model JN-4 "Jenny" biplane. The aircraft was based at a rented field on the north side of town. On the first day of operations, August 25, pilot J.L. Goodrich took eleven passengers—one at a time—up for aerial views of their city. The company's first commercial deliveries were copies of the *Grand Rapids Press*, flown to West Michigan towns by "Fish" Hassell. Lee Woodruff, a college student who assisted in the operation, later became editor of the *Press*.

The field needed considerable leveling before it could be used for takeoffs and landings, and work began with a groundbreaking ceremony on November 26, 1919. Shovels apparently weren't enough for such an important occasion, so Dudley Waters of the Aero Club climbed aboard a tractor to break the turf.

According to a *Herald* report of the event, one of the officials present "stated that he is in correspondence with a large aviation company which is preparing to operate dirigibles from New York to San Francisco, stopping at Chicago, and that he had been asked to provide them a landing place here." But that turned out to be nothing more than a dream.

Roseswift's flights soon proved to be a fleeting fantasy, too. The airline was a bit ahead of its time, and its operations ended in 1921 when the business proved to be unprofitable. During the next four years, there were only two planes flying from the airport.

Meanwhile, on the other side of the state, William B. Stout was moving more and more into the field of flying. He was an engineer who had designed automobiles, and when Packard Motor Company started an aviation division in 1916, he became its first chief engineer. In 1923, when he began experimenting with all-metal aircraft, he established the Stout Metal Airplane Company, which was sold to Ford Motor Company a year later.

At Grand Rapids in 1926, Stout told members of the Rotary Club about his huge all-metal airplanes and his plans to establish a passenger airline that would provide daily flights. One of the cities to be served would be Detroit; the other had not yet been identified.

Grover C. Good, president of the city's chamber of commerce, took Stout to Kent County Airport and suggested that it should be the other

After Kent County's Board of Supervisors approved use of a former fairground and work farm for use as a flying field, members of the Grand Rapids Aero Club gathered at the site in November 1919 for a groundbreaking ceremony. Dudley Waters used a tractor to crack the sod and begin the leveling process. *Courtesy of Grand Rapids History and Special Collections, Archives, Grand Rapids Public Library.*

terminal of his airline. Linking Michigan's two largest cities by air would be a logical move, he said. Stout admitted the possibilities, but he pointed out that a lot of improvements would need to be made at the field. For one thing, many stumps needed to be pulled out, and considerable grading would be necessary. A building for use as an office and terminal would need to be built, too.

Good assured Stout that funds could be raised to make that happen, and members of the Aero Club soon were soliciting donations. About $25,000 would be needed, and the group quickly came up with $20,000. The board of supervisors, recognizing the advantages that an air service of this kind could bring, provided the other $5,000.

In its June 10, 1926 edition, the *Grand Rapids Press* said that work on the field had progressed and that "air service between Grand Rapids and Detroit may begin by the Stout Air Service, Inc., the last week of June or the first week in July." The report added that "most of the work has been grading, and for this improvement gasoline-operated shovels and other excavating equipment have been furnished without charge." Other improvements at the field, according to the *Press*, were the construction of a two-story office building and a gasoline service station.

Progress wasn't as speedy as anticipated, but the August 1 edition of the *Herald* reported a celebration at the airport during the previous day: "Twenty-five thousand persons Saturday afternoon attended the dedication of the Grand Rapids Airport and watched the Stout Ford aeroplane, *Miss Grand Rapids*, leave for Detroit on the first official trip of a schedule which calls for regular passenger, freight, and mail service between the two cities."

In its report on the afternoon of July 31, the *Press* said:

> *With a sky full of visiting planes, roads threaded in every direction, and crowds vying for available space in the aviation field south of the city, commercial air passenger service was begun at Grand Rapids's modern airport Saturday afternoon with the first regularly scheduled flight of the big metal monoplane of the Stout Air Services, Inc., to Detroit...Early in the day the roads to the airport on Madison Avenue showed signs of activity and just previous to the program there was traffic enough to busy all available sheriff's deputies, twenty members of the Grand Rapids Police Department, fifteen state policemen, and fifty Boy Scouts who operated along Madison and Division avenues.*

All didn't come in automobiles, however. Six planes flew in from Selfridge Field at Mount Clemens, and five came from Battle Creek. Other aircraft brought passengers from Muskegon and Kalamazoo. Two airplanes arrived from Detroit, one of them piloted by Eddie Stinson. "Fish" Hassell was one of the passengers on a plane from Dayton, Ohio.

Stout, with the support of Henry Ford, had established Stout Air Service, which operated the new Detroit-Grand Rapids Airline.

It was the first passenger airline in the United States!

According to Earl Spielmacher, a *Grand Rapids Press* photographer with an interest in aviation history, Lansing was Stout's first choice for a terminal to be linked with Detroit, but officials there were less cooperative about making necessary improvements than those in Grand Rapids.

The office and passenger depot at Grand Rapids, according to the *Press*, was a two-story structure of frame construction. The *Herald* noted that it had "a spacious club-house type of waiting room" and "a complete electric kitchen." There also was a room where luggage was weighed. Passengers could carry up

Miss Grand Rapids, the Detroit–Grand Rapids Airline plane that first carried passengers between the two cities in 1927, registered another first a year later when it flew a load of Grand Rapids furniture to the J. L. Hudson store in Detroit. Detroit-Grand Rapids was America's first passenger airline. *Courtesy of Grand Rapids History and Special Collections, Archives, Grand Rapids Public Library.*

to twenty-five pounds with no charge in addition to fare. Costs were eighteen dollars for a one-way ride and thirty-five for a round trip.

At the east end of the line, the planes landed and took off from Ford Airport in Dearborn, described in company literature as "the finest example of what a port should be that exists in this country of ours." That was not an exaggeration. Henry Ford funded its development and, when it opened in 1926, it had the world's first concrete runways. Within a few years, airports at other American cities paved their takeoff and landing strips, but another ten years would pass before concrete runways appeared in Europe.

Planes of the Detroit-Grand Rapids Airline were Stout 2-AT Pullmans—single-engine, high-winged monoplanes that were the first all-metal aircraft certified in the United States. Stout also referred to this model as the Maiden Detroit (made in Detroit), but it was better known as the Tin Goose. It had padded leather seats, a small writing table, windows that opened, a restroom and heating provided by engine exhaust. Eventually it was redesigned to become the 3-AT, an airship with three engines, and then redesigned again to become the well-known Ford Trimotor.

The Tin Geese had wingspans of fifty-four feet and forty-eight-foot-long fuselages covered with corrugated aluminum. Twelve-cylinder engines propelled the 2-ATs to a maximum speed of about a hundred miles per hour. A *Press* feature in 1986, marking the sixtieth anniversary of the first Grand Rapids-Detroit flight, noted, "This was in the day before starters, so the engines had to be 'hand-propped,' a process carried out by two brave souls who started the propeller spinning by hand."

Detroit–Grand Rapids planes carried nearly six thousand passengers 200,000 miles without an accident during their first year. But that also was its last. Henry Ford was not satisfied with financial returns and halted operations almost exactly a year after the big opening ceremony in Grand Rapids. Stout, however, kept operating lines to other cities, but he sold out to United Aircraft and Transport Company two years later. In 1931, UATC was part of a merger that formed United Airlines.

There was hardly a lapse in activity at Kent County Airport, however. In 1927, when Detroit-Grand Rapids planes turned off their engines, a hangar was constructed for aircraft of another line, Furniture Capital Air Service. A year later, airplanes of Thompson Aeronautical Corporation began providing airmail service for Grand Rapids, Muskegon and Kalamazoo.

Another year later, Kohler Aviation Corporation began daily flights between Grand Rapids and Milwaukee, with stops in Muskegon. Its planes were Keystone-Loening amphibians. These rather strange aircraft were commonly called "Ducks" and looked a bit like them. The enclosed cabin, above a large pontoon, had seats for six passengers. However, the pilots sat outside in an open cockpit—not a great place to be while crossing Lake Michigan in rain, sleet and snow.

A major administrative change at the airport in 1930 was the board of supervisors' appointment of Thomas E. Walsh as a full-time manager of the facility. Walsh, who as a boy had skipped school so he could see the first airplane over the city in 1911, had been chairman of the board's Aviation Committee. As manager, he supervised operations at Kent County Airport for nearly thirty years.

There was another celebration at the corner of Madison Avenue and Thirty-second Street in October 1931 when the airport was dedicated as Daniel W. Cassard Field, honoring a Grand Rapids native and pioneer pilot who had given his life in service to his country during World War I.

Kohler Airlines staff members line up alongside one of their Keystone-Loening amphibians at Kent County Airport in the early 1930s. *Courtesy of Grand Rapids History and Special Collections, Archives, Grand Rapids Public Library.*

Spirits on that occasion were dampened a bit by torrential rain, which forced cancellation of an aerial parade over the city by six National Guard planes, as well as those of several local fliers. Also wiped out were plans for an air show featuring stunts, races and a parachute drop.

Nevertheless, a crowd of two thousand turned up at the airport for the dedication, which included unveiling by Boy Scouts of a stone monument with a brass tablet honoring the local hero. Then Leslie P. Kefgen of Bay City, state commander of the American Legion, paid tribute to Cassard. His comments were summarized in a *Herald* article a day later:

> *Commander Kefgen sketched the life history of Lieutenant Cassard, tracing his birth and youth in Grand Rapids, his education at Yale, and then his war training at Fort Sheridan, Illinois, the Royal Flying Corps School at Toronto, and later in Texas before he was sent to France with the pursuit group of the 147th Aero Squadron.*
>
> *The memorable battle of the fatal 16th day of July, 1918, when his plane was shot to earth by ten German ships, was described. When his*

The airport looked like this before improvements and expansions during the 1930s and '40s.

body was found, there was a bullet hole through his heart, indicating he was dead before reaching the ground.

"Perhaps the inscription on this tablet, 'He fell gloriously, fighting to the end,' is the greatest tribute that can be paid to Lieutenant Cassard," said Commander Kefgen.

Despite the rain, younger folk at the dedication seemed to have a great time, the *Herald* noted:

Concluding the dedication program a crowd of boys, ever present when airplanes are the attraction, enjoyed a field day. The legion committee, cooperating with the airport committee, offered free hot dogs and coffee to those attending the dedication. Many of the boys were observed circling the distribution table five or six times.

In following years, as the size and speed of planes and the amount of air traffic increased, the airfield was frequently modified and improved to keep pace.

During the early 1930s, a project of the federal government's Works Progress Administration (WPA) made possible the remodeling of the administration building and construction of a restaurant. Then, in 1939 the administration building was replaced by a new structure with two-foot-thick walls of concrete and steel, which were said to be bombproof. In 1947, a $60,000 project provided a new control tower atop the building.

On the flying field, a need for expansion in 1949 resulted in acquisition of an additional 120 acres on which eighty-nine houses were located. Three years later, the north–south runway was extended to a length of more than a mile. This development required placement of crossing gates at Forty-fourth Street to halt automobile traffic while planes were landing and taking off.

However, further expansion was needed just a few years later, and in 1957 a consultant was hired to advise whether further improvements should be made at the present site or whether operations should move to a new location. A year later, the board of supervisors arranged for development of a master plan for a new airport in Cascade Township. The official transfer of operations from the old airport to the new one took place at midnight on November 23, 1963. But expansion was soon needed there, too, and by 1970, it doubled in size.

In 1999, the impressive facility was named the Gerald R. Ford International Airport, honoring the Grand Rapids area's favorite son.

Meanwhile, the abandoned old airport at Madison Avenue and Thirty-second Street became an industrial park with most of the former runways converted to streets. The principal thoroughfare through the complex is Roger B. Chaffee Boulevard, named in honor of the Grand Rapids astronaut whose life was cut short when fire broke out during a preflight test of the Apollo 1 command module. Astronauts Virgil Grissom and Edward White also died in the tragedy. The principal purpose of the Apollo Program was to land humans on the moon and return them safely to earth. Six of its missions, from 1969 through 1972, succeeded in doing that.

In its information for passengers, the Detroit-Grand Rapids Airline included the following ten items of advice:

HOW TO GET THE MAXIMUM ENJOYMENT OUT OF YOUR FLIGHT

1. Don't Worry.

Relax, settle back, and enjoy life. If there's any worrying to be done, let the pilot do it; that's what he's hired for.

2. The Pilot Always Takes Off and Lands into the Wind.

Be patient while the plane taxis to the corner of the field before taking off. The luxury of flying doesn't appear until you begin to use the third dimension.

3. The Pilot Always Banks the Plane When Turning in the Air.

Just as a race track is banked at the corners, so an airplane is tilted when making a perfect turn. Take the turns naturally with the plane. Don't try to hold the lower wing up with the muscles of the abdomen—it's unfair to yourself and an unjust criticism of your pilot.

4. The Atmosphere Is Like an Ocean.

It supports the plane just as firmly as the ocean supports a ship. At the speed you are traveling, the air has a density practically equivalent to water; to satisfy yourself, put your hand out the window and feel the tremendous pressure. That ever-present pressure is your guarantee of absolute safety.

5. The Wind is Similar to an Ocean Current.

At flying levels it is usually as regular as a great, smooth-flowing river. You can study its direction by watching the shadow of clouds on the country below, or the smoke from chimneys. Once in a while the wind is gusty and rough, like the gulfstream off the coast of Florida. These gusts used to be called "air pockets," but they are nothing more than billows of warm and cool air and nothing to be alarmed over.

6. The Air Pressure Changes with Altitude.

Some people have ears that are sensitive to the slight changes in air density at different altitudes. If so, swallow once in a while, or breathe a little through the mouth, so that the pressure on both sides of the ear drums will be equalized. If you hold your nose and swallow, you will hear a little crack in your ears, caused by the suction of air on the ear drums. Try it.

7. Dizziness is Unknown in Airplanes.

There is no discomfort in looking downwards while flying because there is no connection with the earth; only a sense of confidence and security, similar perhaps to what birds feel. Follow the route on the map, and identify the places you pass. Owing to the altitude, you may think you are moving very slowly, although the normal flying speed of the Stout-Ford plane is 95 miles an hour.

8. When about to Land.

The pilot throttles the engine, preparatory to gliding down to the airport. The engine is not needed in landing, and the plane can be landed perfectly with the engine entirely cut off. From an altitude of 2,500 feet, it is possible to glide, with engine stopped, to any field within a radius of $4^1/_2$ miles. Under no occasion, attempt to open the cabin door until the plane has come to a full stop.

9. The Stout-Ford All-Metal Plane Is the Safest in the World.

Built by the great Ford organization, made entirely of duralumin metal and steel alloys, it is the strongest plane of its type in the world. It is automatically stable. Were the pilot to put it in any position and then release the controls, it would return automatically to the normal flying position.

These planes are now in regular daily use transporting passengers, mail, or goods on air lines operating in Michigan, Indiana, Illinois, Ohio, and Florida. By the end of 1926, they will have flown approximately 750,000 miles—equal to thirty times around the world at the equator!

10. Our Motto is Safety—First, Last, and Always.

In addition to employing only the safest plane, we maintain a daily inspection far more rigorous than any ever given any other form of vehicle. Your pilot is one of the best in the country. An expert motor and plane mechanic flies every trip and is also trained as an alternate pilot. Nothing is omitted that we believe may add to your safety and comfort. Hence we repeat—settle back, or move around as you wish, enjoy the trip, and—

GET THE MAXIMUM ENJOYMENT
OUT OF YOUR FLIGHT!

CHAPTER 9

Lindy Lands

G rand Rapids had never seen the kinds of crowds that turned out when Charles Lindbergh soared into the city with the *Spirit of St. Louis* on August 12, 1927. Presidents and would-be presidents had come to West Michigan and been welcomed by throngs, but none as large or as enthusiastic as the assemblage that welcomed the twenty-five-year-old flier who had conquered the Atlantic just two months earlier.

Crowd estimates of the two local newspapers were confusing and contradictory. In its next edition, the *Grand Rapids Herald*'s page-one banner headline proclaimed, "50,000 Pay Homage to Lindbergh in Ocean Flyer's Day of Triumph Here." It said 25,000 were on hand at the old Kent County Airport for his arrival, and 15,000 were at John Ball Park an hour later when he spoke there. An evening banquet, according to the paper, was attended by 2,000. The *Grand Rapids Press* didn't provide a figure for the airport assembly or the banquet, but its estimate of the crowd at the park was tremendous—100,000.

The Grand Rapids stop was one of ninety-two that Lindbergh made during his three-month tour after the historic journey to Paris. Before he left on that first solo flight across the ocean, multimillionaire Harry Guggenheim told the pilot, "When you get back, look me up." He later admitted he didn't think there was much chance he'd ever see Lindbergh again.

But the flier did get back, and he did look up Guggenheim. And then they arranged the tour funded by Harry and his father, Daniel. On July 20, Lindy zoomed down the runway at Mitchel Field on Long Island, New York, and headed for Hartford, Connecticut, the first stop on the tour that would cover twenty-two thousand miles.

By Wednesday, August 10, he was at Ford Airport in Dearborn and headed for Detroit, his birthplace and the home of his mother, Evangeline Lodge Land Lindbergh, who was a chemistry teacher at Cass Technical High School. She was a niece of John C. Lodge, Detroit councilman and mayor during the 1920s in whose honor Lodge Freeway is named. During her son's transatlantic flight, she had followed his progress on a special telephone link provided by the *Detroit News*.

From the airport, Lindbergh and his mother were escorted to Northwestern field in Detroit by a fleet of thirty-six motorcycle policemen. Half of the sixty thousand at the field to hear him speak were children. Four radio stations aired Lindbergh's comments at the event.

Besides the appearance at the park, Wednesday's activities included an evening banquet at a downtown hotel and an afternoon visit to the house on Forest Avenue where Lindbergh had been born. A bronze plaque was placed there that afternoon to mark the site. However, some city officials didn't think enough of Lindbergh in later years to preserve the historic structure. It was torn down in a 1973 urban renewal project.

Lindbergh's host during his stay in the Detroit area was Henry Ford, and on Thursday the automobile manufacturer and his son, Edsel, both went into the air for the first time when the visiting pilot gave them rides in the *Spirit of St. Louis*.

The acquaintance would lead to an eventual business relationship. During World War II, Ford hired Lindbergh as a technical advisor in the production of B-24 Liberator bombers at his massive Willow Run plant. When less time was needed for his duties there, Lindbergh split his time between the B-24 operations for Ford and the production of F4U Corsair fighters being manufactured for the navy by the Voight Division of United Aircraft Corporation.

After his 1927 stay in Detroit, Lindbergh took off from Ford Airport in Dearborn on Friday and headed for Grand Rapids. So that persons in other cities could get a glimpse of the *Spirit of St. Louis* as it passed overhead, his route took him north to Flint and Saginaw, then southwest over Lansing and Ionia.

Nothing quite like the Lindberghs' visit had ever taken place in the city before. At the mayor's request, factories and some of the banks closed for the afternoon. From 2:00 to 5:00 p.m., the post office shut its doors. Automobiles lined the highways leading into the city. Five planes of the Michigan National Guard's 107th Observation Squadron flew down from Grayling.

Lindy Lands

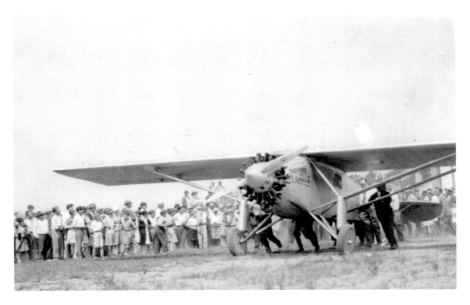

With part of the huge crowd at Kent County Airport in the background, field hands push the *Spirit of St. Louis* to a safe resting place after Lindbergh's arrival on August 12, 1927. *Courtesy of Grand Rapids History and Special Collections, Archives, Grand Rapids Public Library.*

Among the pilots of those aircraft was Lieutenant Harry H. Ogden, one of eight U.S. Army Air Service fliers who, in 1924, took off from Seattle in four planes and headed westward to make the first round-the-world flight. One of their four Douglas World Cruiser planes crashed into a mountain on the second day of flying. The other three continued, crossing Asia and Europe, but the plane in which Ogden was one of the fliers was forced down in the Atlantic and sank while being towed by a ship that had picked up the pilots. In Nova Scotia, they boarded a substitute aircraft, and the three planes flew on to Seattle. The circuit of the earth took 175 days.

Lindbergh's Grand Rapids welcomers began assembling at Kent County Airport before noon on August 12, 1927, and the plane soared into view right on time at 2:00 p.m. The *Spirit of St. Louis*, according to the *Herald*, was "silvery and delicate looking as she first appeared in the distant heavens, came circling over the landing field, whirred over the heads of the crowd once or twice and dropped easily to the south end of the landing field, flirted the dust in the air for a second and came taxiing into the hangar."

An hour earlier, however, there had been a surprise when a big Ford-Stout Trimotor passenger plane landed. Among those who descended from the aircraft was Lindbergh's mother. She had advised Grand Rapids officials that morning that she would be in the city when its citizens honored her son. In its Saturday edition, the *Herald* reported what happened as evening approached on Friday:

> *Eluding his escort of motor cars and police, Col. Charles A. Lindbergh Friday afternoon slipped into the Pantlind Hotel, obtained his favorite camera, and with his mother, Congressman Carl E. Mapes, Mrs. Mapes, and Mayor Elvin Swarthout went to the local airport, climbed into the Spirit of St. Louis with his mother as passenger and sailed over Grand Rapids…Mrs. Lindbergh had been up with her son before, but never in the craft which spanned the Atlantic.*

After his welcome at the airport, Lindbergh and many of those present left for John Ball Park. Crowds lined the streets as they headed down Madison Avenue to State Street, then to Jefferson Avenue, Fulton Street, Monroe Street, Bridge Street, Straight Avenue, back to Fulton and into the park.

At the corner of Madison Avenue and Burton Street, Lindbergh saw the Grand Rapids Railroad's electric coach that had been named in his honor. When the procession reached Campau Square, the Commercial Driver Club Band played marches as its members stood on a balcony of the Pantlind Hotel; and at John Ball Park, the Grand Rapids Press Newsboys' Band provided the music.

Twelve crippled children who had been participants in the parade joined other youngsters at the park in a special section that had been reserved for them. The *Herald*'s reporter wrote:

> *In spite of the fact that all the athletic field and the hills at the back of the field were packed with people, there was an intimate touch to the scene lacking in the other tributes of the day, and the crowds, with children in the front ranks, let loose in wilder cheering than was heard elsewhere.*

No matter whether the crowd at the park was 15,000 as the *Herald* reported or 100,000 as the *Press* estimated, it was a grand affair. As Lindbergh spoke, his words were heard not only by those present but also by thousands of others who listened on radios in their homes. Since airports in those days were not as plentiful or as well maintained as now—some planes still were flying from farmers' fields—the guest of honor stressed the need for more and better facilities:

We need two things to place aviation in its proper place as an industry of the nation and to place the United States in the proper place among the nations of the world. First, cooperation of the people, and secondly we need airports. Airports are as necessary in the promotion of aviation as good roads are to the automobile. The best way to promote aeronautics in a given city is to establish a well-equipped airport in which case the city will be visited frequently by aircraft.

The events of the day were not without a few problems. The *Herald* reported that a gang of pickpockets preyed on crowds at both the airport and the park. "Almost $1,000 was reported as having been taken," the paper said, "and police believe that much more, which was unreported, was obtained by the thieves."

There was big trouble that night, too. "A mob of several thousand persons stormed the Grand Rapids Airport last night," the *Herald* said, "and for a time threatened to break from the control of police and demolish the *Spirit of St. Louis*." However, reinforcements were called in and the crowd was brought under control.

That night, Lindbergh's mother returned to Detroit in the trimotor that had brought her to Grand Rapids, and hundreds were at the airport to see her off. Lindbergh was among them, of course.

The plane left at 10:00 p.m., and in those days there were no lights at the airport. So, before the aircraft took off, an automobile raced to the far side of the field, swung around at the end of the runway, and aimed its lights in the direction of the plane. That provided a bit of illumination as well as an indication of where the runway ended. The trimotor was soon in the air and, according to the *Press*, turned on its two big lights.

On Saturday, Lindbergh left for Chicago, the next stop on his tour. After his takeoff, he circled the field twice and then headed north over the city. From downtown, he swung to the east and soared over Sunshine Hospital on Fuller Avenue as a treat for patients there. Forty minutes later, he was over Kalamazoo and then passed Benton Harbor and St. Joseph to give folks there the thrill of seeing the *Spirit of St. Louis* soar overhead.

After a couple days at Chicago, he headed westward across the northern states to Seattle, then down the Pacific coast to San Diego. From there he crossed southern states to Jacksonville and then flew up the Atlantic coast to New York City. The ninety-three-day tour involved 260 hours and 45 minutes of flying time. The *Spirit of St. Louis* flew over all forty-eight of the country's states of that time. The last leg of the tour was a flight from Philadelphia back to Mitchel Field, Long Island, on October 23, 1927.

In December, Lindbergh took off on another tour, this one to thirteen Latin American countries.

After his return from Paris in 1927, he had been welcomed by a tremendous ticker-tape parade in New York City and then by President Calvin Coolidge at Washington, D.C.

The White House was undergoing renovation, so a special dinner in his honor was held in the Patterson House at 15 Du Pont Circle, temporary home of the Coolidges, on June 11. Among those present was David Morrow, a businessman and politician who had been an Amherst College classmate of the president. After World War I, Coolidge chose him to head a board to make recommendations regarding the country's aviation policy. One of its suggestions resulted in establishment of the U.S. Army Air Corps in 1926.

After becoming ambassador to Mexico in October 1927, Morrow asked Lindbergh to tour Latin America as he had the United States. The flier agreed and started the tour on December 13, 1927, with a non-stop flight from Washington, D.C., to Mexico City. After touching down in several countries, he returned with another nonstop flight, Havana to St. Louis on February 14, 1928.

Lindbergh spent Christmas of 1927 with the family of Ambassador Morrow in Mexico City. The Morrows' daughter Anne, a senior at Smith College in Massachusetts, was home for the holidays; and the Morrows also invited Lindbergh's mother to be with them for the holiday. She flew from Ford Airport at Dearborn to Mexico City in a Ford Trimotor made available by Henry Ford.

The plane, a model 4-AT-A with a U.S. registration number of C-1077, was flown by Lindbergh while it was in Mexico and later was piloted by several other notable fliers including aviatrix Amelia Earhart. The aircraft is still flyable and is one of about thirty planes at the Golden Wings Museum in Blaine, Minnesota.

On the day after Christmas, Lindbergh took the controls of the plane to give the Morrow family and several associates a view of Mexico City from above. The largest passenger load was one of fifteen wives and children of embassy staff members. On another flight, Mexican Minister of War Joaquin Amaro and his wife were aboard. However, in Lindbergh's future, the most important occupants of the cabin that day would prove to be Mrs. Morrow and her children, Con, Elisabeth and Anne.

It was Anne who caught his attention—and he, hers.

This was her first flight, and she was fascinated—both by the thrill of soaring through the air and the flier who made it possible. "It was a complete and intense experience," she wrote in her diary. "I will not be happy till it happens again."

Soon after Ambassador Morrow announced the engagement of Anne to Lindbergh at the embassy on February 12, 1929, the pilot was back in Mexico and the courting couple took off together from Mexico City's Valbuena Airport for a flight over a nearby volcano. Before returning, they landed at another field and, upon taking off again, a wheel fell off the plane. Back at Valbuena, Lindbergh's attempt to crash-land with just one wheel appeared to be successful on touchdown, but after about thirty feet, the aircraft flipped over. Anne and Charles had to be pulled from the cabin window, but there weren't life-threatening injuries. He had a dislocated shoulder and a sprained wrist, and she suffered shock.

There were many happier times in the air for the couple. Anne, too, became captivated by the thrill of flying, and Charles gave her lessons. Eventually, she also became an accomplished flier. She flew solo in 1929, became the first woman to get a glider pilot's license in 1930 and received a private pilot's license in 1931.

After their wedding in May 1929, much of their time was spent in the air. Anne was Charles's co-pilot on exciting journeys that took them all over the world and provided the ingredients for fulfillment of her other passion—writing.

Their life together was marred by difficulties—almost constant invasion of their privacy by reporters and photographers, the kidnapping and murder of an infant son, the turmoil resulting from their views concerning Nazi Germany before America was drawn into World War II—but their devotion to one another continued throughout their lifetimes.

CHAPTER 10

Mom's Ride Home

After Grand Rapids Herald *reporter J. Francis McCarthy joined Evangeline Lindbergh on her night flight back to Detroit in a Ford Trimotor plane, he filed this page-one feature for the August 12, 1927 edition of the paper.*

HERALD REPORTER DESCRIBES PLEASURES OF NIGHT FLIGHT OF MRS. LINDBERGH'S PARTY

By J. Francis McCarthy, *Herald* Staff Reporter

Three tons of metal rushing through the moonlight at an average speed of 100 miles an hour featured the first cross country night flight ever attempted by the Stout Air Services Inc., which was combined Friday night with the official au revoir of Mrs. Evangeline L.L. Lindbergh, who rode the three-motored Ford-Stout plane to her home in Detroit after sharing during the day in the plaudits heaped by Grand Rapids on her illustrious son, Col. Charles A. Lindbergh.

Ideal flying weather favored this trip, which proved not only the possibilities of night flying but also the safety of this undertaking, while the party, especially Mrs. Lindbergh, marveled at the appearance of a Michigan landscape illuminated by the pale rays of the moon and an occasional beacon creeping through the windows of scattered farm houses.

A trimotor like this one at Ford Airport in Dearborn carried Lindbergh's mother to Grand Rapids where she took her first ride in the *Spirit of St. Louis*. Her return flight to southeast Michigan was on the same plane and was a night flight. Since Kent County Airport then was unlighted, an automobile similar to the one pictured drove to the end of the field and aimed its lights back down the runway toward the the plane. *Courtesy of Superior View, Marquette, Michigan.*

Beside Mrs. Lindbergh, the ship carried Mr. and Mrs. William B. Stout of Detroit; Glenn Hoppin, secretary of the Stout Air Services; Harold E. Cummings, of Napanee, Ont., nephew of Mr. Stout; Andrew Massamer, Ford mechanic; a Detroit newspaperman; and the writer. Capt. C.D. Swenson was at the controls.

Unswerving faith in night as well as day flying was voiced by Col. Lindbergh, who spent about a quarter of an hour with the passengers while the motors were being warmed up just previous to the takeoff from the Grand Rapids Airport at 10 p.m. Asked by Mr. Stout whether he wished a wire informing him of his mother's arrival at Detroit, the flying colonel replied:

"Don't bother about that. There isn't a doubt but what you will make it safely. And if you don't, I'll hear about it sooner."

As soon as Lindy stepped out, the giant plane roared across the field and with no effort nosed toward the heavens. With a gradual climb, it circled the field in a mother's farewell to her son and headed for her destination.

Reaching an altitude of 2,000 feet, the plane was leveled and the passengers gazed at a sight which must be seen to be appreciated. The ground loomed far below in a grayish hue, interrupted by the weaving of automobile headlights around invisible highways. A world upside down might to some extent describe the scene.

Automobile lights and the widely separated farmhouse beacons could have served for stars, while the reflection of the moon in scattered ponds and streams carried out the lunar effect, with the lighter gray of newly plowed fields contrasted with timber sections appearing as clouds to complete the celestial arrangement.

Forty minutes from the takeoff brought the plane above Lansing, where the lighted capitol dome stood out in bold relief. Boulevard lights were set along even rows, while an occasionally extra bright traffic semaphore could be seen changing from green to red. But the giant bird sped through the night like an object from another world, unhindered by mere traffic laws of the earth below.

Hardly had the state capital been left behind when a new version of night flying was presented to the party. A row of clouds was directly in the path of, and at the same level with, the ship, but the pilot nosed her again towards the heavens. She passed through the near end of this obstruction, which seemed more like a dense and damp fog, and then surmounted it, obscuring the sight of ground, but replacing it with an appearance of snowbanks, augmented by the reflection of the moon.

For the rest of the journey the ground seemed slightly blurred with intermittent openings, through which the sights of the first part of the trip were repeated.

Not once during the ride did Mrs. Lindbergh mention herself or her son and, when questions were put to her, she cautiously avoided them, interrupting with a remark about the present voyage. It was her first night flight, too, and even rides with the famous Lindy couldn't take her mind off the present. But the manner in which she enjoyed the new thrill gave undeniable proof of the source of the Lone Eagle's Iron nerve and love for the air.

Talking to any great extent, however, was extremely difficult, due to the roar of the triple motors. In this latter phase, the passengers were given a slight example of what Lindy went through in trying to remain awake during his memorable flight. After some time up, the roar gradually worked into a constant drone which, coupled with the darkness and vibration of the machine, offers one of the best inducements for sleep.

Intermittent rays of light being cast at regular intervals on the plane, brought to the passengers the first indication that the journey was at an end.

In the distance could be seen the illuminated outline of the Ford airport, while a revolving beacon drew the attention of the pilot.

The altitude, which during the trip ranged from 2,000 feet to nearly a mile, was lowered while the 100-mile-an-hour speed was cut down. The 12-passenger air limousine drifted toward earth, and with a slight bound landed at its destination, just one hour and 35 minutes from the takeoff. The plane was taxied into position in the Ford hangar and came to a halt between an especially built Ford product, the smallest plane built, on one side, and the three-motored "Josephine Ford," the plane in which Richard E. Byrd circled the North Pole, on the other.

Passengers and operators stepped out, and another chapter in Michigan aircraft history was written.

CHAPTER 11

Fairs and Circuses, Comings and Goings

During the early years of powered flight over Grand Rapids, just the sound of one of the magnificent flying machines was enough to turn all eyes skyward. But the biggest thrills were yet to come. And they did when special events started happening and special people began arriving and departing at Kent County Airport. Thousands came to see scores of aircraft that made stops during air tours; planes and pilots that generated thrills at air fairs and circuses; and dignitaries who, a few years earlier, would have come and gone by train.

One of the first of these special occasions unfolded on May 9, 1919, when six army planes landed at the airport during a tour intended to generate military recruits and solicit contributions for the government's Victory Loan campaign. The aircraft started out from Selfridge Field at Mount Clemens and made their first stop at Jackson. From Grand Rapids, they would go on to Battle Creek, Kalamazoo, Holland, Grand Haven and Muskegon.

Five of the planes carried a passenger as well as the pilot. Two of them were mechanics, and the other three were Grand Rapids newspaper reporters. One was Henry P. Zuidema of the *Grand Rapids Press*, who quoted the commander of Selfridge Field as saying that "flights to Traverse City, Cadillac, and Alma cannot be considered." That, he added, was because "the distance is too great for the planes, and flights over miles of wooded land in northern Michigan counties might result disastrously if attempted."

Zuidema waxed a bit poetic in the description of his airborne experience:

On this flight, I have learned what must make the birds sing. My conclusion was reached soon after we rose into the air at Selfridge Field. Forgetting "earthly" annoyances, I felt as a lark must feel flying high above sweeping, green meadows and flirting with fleecy clouds. "This is the life." I thought, and if my lips uttered no sound, my heart at least was singing.

His tone became less placid as he proceeded:

After we had reached what I considered a bewildering height, but which did not seem to be anything unusual to my pilot, we took a downward swoop; and I tried to imagine I was riding on the roller coaster at Ramona and, incidentally, wishing I was just as safe...

After I had grown comparatively accustomed to the scenes below, I tried to imagine how I would feel if I were flying over German trenches. I pictured a battle with one or a half dozen enemy planes. For the present, I concluded, my thrills were sufficient.

But he appeared willing to consider the possibility of greater thrills in the future and ended his story by saying, "I am willing to say right now that in the next war I'm going into the aviation service."

Planes from Selfridge Field flew to Grand Rapids again in March 1927 as part of a welcoming celebration for polar explorer Richard Byrd, who also came by plane. During May 1926, Byrd and pilot Floyd Bennett flew to the north pole—an accomplishment that excited folks of that time nearly as much as the *Apollo 11* mission to the moon did more recently.

Among others at the airport to welcome Byrd, an officer in the U.S. Navy, was Grand Rapids resident Joseph McCain, who had served in the Union navy during the Civil War and, in 1927, was commodore of the National Association of Naval Veterans.

In comparing the explorer's flight to Grand Rapids from Detroit with his historic journey of the year before, the *Press* said, "When he embarked on that flight that has given him an immortal leadership among the great explorers, he was flying to what might mean the end that had befallen other intrepid men in that barren stretch."

As Commander Byrd stepped from the Ford Trimotor that had carried him from Detroit, the South High School Band provided a triumphal accompaniment. Then three of the army pilots thrilled the welcoming crowd as they zoomed their pursuit planes through an exhibition of combat tactics. "The spectators got their greatest thrill," the *Press* said, "not from the spins nor from the loops but from the straight drop of the winged craft until it seemed they surely would crash into the ground."

When the performance ended, a parade of automobiles carried dignitaries to downtown Grand Rapids; and from the corner of Sheldon Avenue and Fulton Street, the Press Newsboy Band led the way to the Pantlind Hotel at Monroe Avenue and Pearl Street. After a dinner and reception there, Byrd showed and described motion pictures of his expedition during an evening program at the city's armory.

The next excitement at the airport came three months after Byrd's visit when planes participating in a national air tour sponsored by Edsel Ford made a stop at Grand Rapids. Fliers started out from Ford Airport in Dearborn on June 27 and eventually soared east to Boston, west to Omaha and south to Dallas. The stop in Grand Rapids was arranged by the Grand Rapids Flying Club, and the planes flew in from Hammond, Indiana, on July 12.

While at the airport, they were serviced and refueled, and lunch was served to the pilots, mechanics and others involved with the tour. Pilots then went to their planes at the edge of the landing field where they explained the merits of their aircraft and answered questions from members of the crowd who had paid a twenty-five-cent admission charge. Those who wished an aerial view had opportunities to go up in planes of Stout Air Services and the flying club.

The biggest crowds and the greatest thrill during the early years of airport activity, of course, came a month later when Lindbergh landed at Grand Rapids.

The first Michigan Air Tour in June 1929 brought another fleet of planes to Kent County Airport despite stormy weather. A page-one story in the *Press* described the situation at Grand Rapids:

> *Perhaps the greatest thrill of the afternoon to the crowds waiting in the rain was to watch the speeding planes high in the gray sky and suddenly see all around them great jagged streaks of lightning and hear the booming of the thunder that made the roar of the planes sound faint by comparison.*
>
> *But no lightning, thunder, rain nor wind that strained some of the planes to the peak of their operating powers was to stop the Michigan Air Tour.*
>
> *Cars were parked three and four deep entirely across the space east from the Flying Club hangar, and another long line of machines stretched across the west end of the port. Boys and girls and men and women ploughed*

about in the water and mud. No mere rain could keep them from the field to see the great airplane show which rewarded their coming.

After the touring aviators landed, a banquet for four hundred persons was provided in the Furniture Capital Air Service hangar. The Press Newsboy Band furnished the music, and Governor Fred W. Green confessed nervousness about his flight to the airport in a trimotor plane and his rosy view of aviation's likely future contributions:

The legendary man who rode on the wings of the wind never had a ride at all. He should have had a ride in a Ford Trimotor plane. I sat beside the pilot and thought about my family and hoped for the best.

I don't believe there are very many of us who realize it when we make real progress. We are talking about passenger and freight service by air. We are talking about a time when we won't have to build roads and pay a gasoline tax.

The *Press* reported that Bert "Fish" Hassell had been invited to the event "but had said he expected to hop off for Sweden early in June."

Among the planes participating in the tour was the Keystone-Loening amphibian of Furniture Capital Air Service. It had taken its first passengers aloft on Memorial Day, flying from the Lake Michigan shore at Grand Haven. The *Press* said it would continue service at Grand Haven throughout the summer. The aircraft was the first of its kind in West Michigan, but a few of the amphibians were providing service across Lake Erie, linking Detroit and Cleveland, and others would soon be flying across Lake Michigan to provide service between Grand Rapids and Milwaukee.

Next to dazzle the aviation thrill seekers at Grand Rapids was the Furniture Capital Air Fair, sponsored by the Grand Rapids Flying Club and the Association of Commerce in September 1929. Billed as the "first air circus ever staged in Grand Rapids," it featured races and other competitive events as well as aerial stunts by thirty-two southern Michigan pilots.

Several thousand persons attended despite a late afternoon drizzle on the first of the fair's two days, which forced cancellation of a night flying exhibition. The afternoon events went off without a hitch, except for a triple parachute jump by Ted Sweet, a local one-legged jumper. His pilot, Floyd Becker, returned to the landing field when mist began to obscure visibility.

An aerial parade of planes over the city opened another air fair in August 1930, and landings of the aircraft were timed to coincide with the arrival at the airport of the event's Queen of the Air, Peggy Schuler. Earlier in the day, Miss Schuler welcomed the Cherry Queen, Signe Holmer and Miss Traverse City, Anna May York, who flew in from northern Michigan. Miss Schuler had been at Milwaukee earlier in the week and invited a group from that city to attend the fair. They made the trip in one of the Keystone-Loening amphibians.

Events of the fair included looping and bomb-dropping contests, races, glider demonstrations and parachute jumps. A special feature at the end of the first day's program, according to a *Press* report, was "a sham battle between the Howitzer Company of the 126th Infantry and pilots of the Furniture Capital Air Service."

A July 1934 fair at the airport opened with another parade of planes, and before landing, thirteen aircraft dropped bombs on a target at the field.

Besides watching the usual competitive events and aerial exhibitions, those who attended had a chance to inspect an unusual airplane built by William Clinger of Grandville. It was a "pusher" byplane with the propeller behind the cabin and pointed to the rear. More typical "tractor" planes have the propeller at the front pulling the plane.

Vera Hull of Grand Rapids went up in a plane for the first time at the fair—and, while aloft, married navy veteran Leonard Schoffner. They boarded the plane in front of the grandstand and repeated their vows as it soared over the field. When they landed, they were given wedding gifts of furniture.

Most spectacular of the air fairs and flying circuses at Kent County Airport during the early years of aviation at Grand Rapids was the Fordon-Brown Air Show in June 1937. Members of the touring group were some of America's best-known speed and stunt pilots. The *Grand Rapids Herald* told about them in its June 20 edition:

> *If it's speed you want to see, you will have a chance to see what 350 miles per hour looks like. Roger Don Rae, 1937 national racing champion, puts his tiny power plane through its paces...*
>
> *Buddy Batzel does two parachute jumps. Saturday, on his test jump to test the direction and force of the wind, he left the ship at 4,000 feet...Buddy's second jump is made from 12,000 feet. He falls for more than two miles before pulling the rip cord of his chute; and even from this great altitude and after this great drop, he makes a spot landing within a few feet of the announcer's stand...*
>
> *Perhaps the greatest bit of flying is done by C.W. Whittenbeck, who does the dreaded and difficult outside loop. There are few pilots who dare this*

feat and none who can approach the master in its execution. His prolonged upside-down flying is of tremendous interest, particularly when he goes across the field upside-down at altitudes of less than 100 feet.

Charles Abel takes to the air in a glider towed by a plane, gains an altitude of about 4,000 feet, and then puts this motorless ship, weighing less than 800 pounds, through all the paces...

Bob O'Dell takes to the air with his stunt ship, turns on the smoke and proceeds to engrave in the blue some weird and colorful designs in smoke...

Harold Johnson takes a six-ton Ford Trimotor ship into the air and does things with it that the designer certainly never figured his ship would be called upon to do. He loops it below an altitude of 600 feet, landing it on one wheel, does rolls, and has the crowd gasping.

Besides thrills, there was comedy. Dick Granere, in the role of Colonel Throttlebottom, went up in a Curtiss pusher. His knowledge of flying is said to be limited to what he has learned from books—and he never read the last chapter.

"He just misses fences," the *Herald* said, "glides over the tops of hangars, gets all tangled up in a loop, decides once to climb out of the plane in mid-air only to change his mind, and does a hundred laughable gyrations that keep the crowd roaring and helps break that nervous tension."

Announcer Hugh Thomasson at the microphone of the public address system kept up an informative and interesting commentary throughout the performances.

Just three weeks before flying at Grand Rapids, Rae crashed his plane while racing at St. Louis. In a story with a May 29 dateline, the Associated Press reported:

A spectacular crash landing by Roger Don Rae, champion American racing pilot, chilled 12,000 spectators today at St. Louis Air Show but the young Lansing, Mich., flier escaped serious injury in the smashup of his tiny monoplane.

Losing half his propeller as he roared close to the ground at 250 miles per hour toward a pylon in front of a gasping grandstand, Rae jerked his plane up to 200 feet, fighting hard for control. It fluttered and came down hard to a belly landing on the airport.

An ambulance and fire trucks raced across the field. Spectators streamed toward the plane which lay with its nose and undercarriage smashed. Rae was treated for severe head cuts.

Skywriter O'Dell was another aviator from Lansing.

After thrilling air show crowds with his parachute jumps, Batzel became a pilot for Eastern Airlines. At the time of his death in 1993 at age eighty-one, his daughter said he left home at the age of fifteen and made parachute jumps in the United States and Europe before performing with the Fordon-Brown group.

Before he died in 1987, Whittenbeck became one of ten outstanding fliers named Silver Eagles by the Experimental Aircraft Association, according to his son, who added that he held the world record for inverted flying, going as low as three feet above the ground upside down. During World War II, he was a flight instructor.

Abel's glider was a departure from the normal. A biplane with typical airplane landing gear, the motorless aircraft looked like a powered plane in flight. At the time of the air show in Grand Rapids, he held the world record with forty-two consecutive loops in a powerless plane. After being towed to a release point nearly a mile up, he would perform a series of loops until about five hundrd feet above the ground, then dive and land in front of the grandstand.

After his tricks with trimotors, Johnson ferried planes across the Atlantic to England during the early years of World War II. Then he took a less hazardous job testing B-24 Liberator bombers that were built at Ford's Willow Run plant. Before the end of the war, he also tested P-38 pursuit planes. In the early 1980s, Johnson flew a plane in an episode of CBS television's *WKRP in Cincinnati*.

During the forty-four years of aviation activity just south of the intersection of Madison Avenue and Thirty-second Street, planes brought hundreds of prominent passengers as well as pilots. Some bearers of big names who stepped off planes at Kent County Airport were adventurers like Richard Byrd, who came in 1927. Others were stars of stage and screen, such as comedians Bud Abbott and Lou Costello, who appeared with a cast of thirty-five for a performance at the Civic Auditorium in 1946.

There were interesting departures as well. In 1947, for example, the Grand Rapids Chicks boarded a plane at the airport and flew to Wisconsin where they battled the Racine Belles for the All-American Girls Professional Baseball League (AAGPBL) Playoff Championship.

The Chicks were one of the AAGPBL's six teams when they moved to Grand Rapids from Milwaukee in 1945. The league had been founded in 1943 by Chicago Cubs owner Philip K. Wrigley, who feared the departure of many major league players for military service might empty ballparks.

Opposite, top: When comedians Bud Abbott and Lou Costello brought their laugh show to the Civic Auditorium in 1946, they paused with members of their crew, cast and orchestra for a photo in front of the plane in which they arrived. *Courtesy of Grand Rapids History and Special Collections, Archives, Grand Rapids Public Library.*

Opposite, bottom: Grand Rapids Chicks manager Johnny Rawlings and several of his players wave to the crowd at Kent County Airport before taking off for Racine, where they continued 1947 playoff competition. Mildred Earp, hero of the seventh-game victory that gave the Chicks the All-American Girls Professional Baseball League (AAGPBL) championship, is third from the right. *Courtesy of Grand Rapids History and Special Collections, Archives, Grand Rapids Public Library.*

Above: Before flying to Racine, the Chicks posted a 2–1 lead in the first three games of the 1947 AAGPBL playoffs at Grand Rapids. This photo of action in one of those games shows Teeny Petras of the Chicks being run down between third base and home plate. *Courtesy of Grand Rapids History and Special Collections, Archives, Grand Rapids Public Library.*

Exploits of the league's teams were fictionalized in the 1992 movie *A League of Their Own*, starring Tom Hanks, Madonna, Geena Davis and Rosie O'Donnell.

The only AAGPBL team to make the playoffs every year, the Chicks advanced to the 1947 finals by eliminating the South Bend Blue Sox in five contests. Racine moved up by topping the Muskegon Lassies in three of their four semifinal games.

The first three games of the finals at Grand Rapids all went into extra innings, and when the action shifted to Racine, the Chicks had a 2–1 edge. After flying to Racine, they won the first game and lost the next two, evening the series. Then, in the decisive seventh game, pitcher Mildred Earp hurled a five-hit shutout for a 1–0 Grand Rapids victory and the championship.

She also batted in the winning run on a really fluky play. In the seventh inning, Jeep Stoll walked and stole second. Doris Tetzlaff sacrificed her to third. Earp attempted to squeeze her home with a bunt but popped up the ball. With Stoll dashing for the plate, it should have been an easy, unassisted double play for Racine's third baseman—if she'd made the catch and dashed back to the bag. But she overran the ball. Another Belles player scooped it up and threw to first, retiring Earp. Meanwhile, Stoll crossed the plate for the game's only score. So it was a happy flight back to Grand Rapids for the Chicks!

CHAPTER 12

Whispering Wings

I t was shortly after 1:00 a.m.—1:19, to be exact—when the first American assault glider, towed by a two-engine transport plane, roared down the runway at Aldermaston Airbase in southern England and headed for the coast of Normandy. This was D-Day, and the assault on Nazi-occupied Europe was underway.

The Waco CG-4A gliders, and the Douglas C-47 Skytrain transport planes that pulled them, could hardly be described as impressive. They were nothing like the sleek and speedy fighters or the powerful bombers that had been pounding targets on the continent. The C-47s had earned the affectionate, though unglamorous, designation "Gooney Birds." The gliders, large but boxlike in appearance, were known to those who flew in them as "Canvas Coffins."

Though rather ugly, the CG4-A was a scary war machine. Flying into combat in one of them was equally frightening. Small arms fire could easily pierce the fabric that covered the welded steel frame of the fuselage; and coming down in a CG4-A was, at best, a controlled crash landing.

The wings, at least, of the motorless aircraft were imposing. They had a span of more than eighty-three feet.

And many of them had come off assembly lines in Grand Rapids.

When the United States was caught up in the conflict that threatened freedom throughout the world, the nation's industries converted the tools that had made automobiles, appliances and furniture for use in the production of planes, tanks, guns and ammunition. Among the West Michigan companies

The flimsiness of Waco CG-4A gliders is apparent in this picture of one of the aircraft being assembled for display at the Fighting Falcon Military Museum in Greenville during 2004. The wood and metal tubing, visible here, was simply covered with canvas. *Courtesy of Antxon Basurko.*

that retooled and reeducated their workers to help the war effort were several Grand Rapids furniture makers.

Wings of some aircraft were still made of wood, and that's something with which the city's furniture fashioners had been working for a century. When the Stinson Division of Vultee Aircraft Corporation needed plywood wings for observation planes, it turned to Grand Rapids. A consortium of thirteen furniture companies, known as Grand Rapids Industries, was formed; and Frederick H. Mueller was named its president. At that time, he was president of one of the member companies, Mueller Furniture, and later he served as secretary of commerce in the administration of President Dwight Eisenhower. In 1944, as Mueller was directing the efforts of Grand Rapids workers to provide parts for planes of the Allies, Eisenhower, as supreme Allied commander, was planning D-day operations.

With Hitler in control of nearly the entire continent of Europe and the Allies preparing for what would be the world's greatest military assault, mass production of gliders for the invasion became a top priority. One of the leading manufacturers affiliated with Cessna Aircraft Company for production of the Waco gliders was Gibson Refrigerator Company at Greenville, just to the northeast of Grand Rapids; and Grand Rapids Industries produced wings for the gliders made there and elsewhere.

An April 1943 article, "Gliders from the Wolverine State," in *Modern Plastics* magazine noted, "Recently some complete gliders have been produced at Grand Rapids, but the largest volume is in the flow of parts from the participating furniture factories into the Grand Rapids Industries plant and out again to Wichita." Among the parts made by the consortium were the mammoth wings. The factory of Imperial Furniture Company, largest of the group, was the site of final assembly for the wings and other large parts of the gliders.

Before the end of the war in 1945, sixteen principal U.S. manufacturers with help from more than a hundred subcontractors built 13,909 CG4-As. Gibson Refrigerator made 1,078 of the gliders at Greenville, and Ford Motor Company assembled 4,190 at its plant near Iron Mountain.

Each of the CG4-As could carry thirteen soldiers, or five men and a jeep, or two GIs and a 105-millimeter howitzer. The cleverly designed, curved, plexiglass-covered nose of the aircraft was hinged at the top to permit front loading and unloading of heavy equipment. In crashes that might propel a jeep or cannon forward, the entire nose and cockpit, with the two pilots belted in their seats, was intended to swing up and out of the way.

One of the Greenville CG4-As was scheduled to take the number one position in the 101st Airborne Division's D-Day glider assault against the Germans in occupied France. It had been paid for by the city's residents in response to appeals from local students. Hoping to raise $17,000 to pay for one of the gliders being built in their town, youngsters from Greenville schools sold war bonds and stamps. The older folks responded in a big way, purchasing $72,000 in bonds—enough to buy four gliders.

To celebrate the accomplishment, Mayor Oscar Rasmussen proclaimed May 19, 1943, "Glider Day." Stores and schools closed their doors, and the high school band led a parade to Black Athletic Field, where one of the gliders was the main attraction. Directly behind the band marched eight students, each of whom had sold more than $1,000 in bonds. During the ceremonies at the field, Greenville's students were presented with the U.S. Treasury Department's Distinguished Service Certificate; and Sally Church, a high school junior, christened the aircraft the *Fighting Falcon*.

Two weeks later, it was disassembled, crated and shipped to England.

U.S. military officials, impressed by the students' efforts and the support of Greenville citizens, ordered that this would be the aircraft to lead the D-Day glider assault. At the controls of the aircraft would be Colonel

This replica of the Waco CG-4A glider that had been selected to lead the D-Day invasion of Europe by Allied forces is one of many fascinating displays at the Kalamazoo Air Zoo. The original was christened by a Greenville High School girl who, with other students, sold enough war bonds and stamps to pay for four of the aircraft. *Courtesy of Kalamazoo Air Zoo.*

Mike Murphy, America's highest-ranking glider pilot. As a barnstorming stuntsman, he had landed planes upside down on wheels attached to upper wings. His assignment was to train glider pilots in Indiana, and he had no obligation to participate in combat. But he talked his way into the D-Day invasion so he could learn how gliders performed in battle. Also aboard the glider would be Brigadier General Donald F. Pratt and his aide, along with their jeep.

Virtually all of the early accounts of D-Day's airborne operations indicate that the *Flying Falcon* was the first to take off, but later data shows the *Falcon* was removed from the lead position and actually was the forty-fifth of Mission Chicago's fifty-two gliders to fly.

As with many war stories, there are varying accounts of what happened—both before takeoff and after. Some say it was decided that a glider with a steel plate beneath the fuselage was needed for protection of the general.

Some say Murphy decided to replace the original *Falcon* with a glider that had a Griswold Nose, a crash protection device. At any rate, the switch in gliders was made prior to the mission. Some sources note that a hasty paint job made the new number one glider look the same as its predecessor.

Gliders, with just fabric covering their metal tubes and wood components, were comparatively light aircraft. Addition of a steel plate, of course, would make a glider heavier and faster in its landing descent. This may have contributed to the failure of Murphy's lead glider to stop when he made a perfect landing in a French pasture. Another problem was that he didn't know the grass in the field was wet—and slippery.

When he hit the brakes, the craft skidded seven hundred yards and smashed into trees. The general and Murphy's copilot were killed. At least one report says the general died from a broken neck. Others state he was crushed when the jeep, which had been anchored behind his seat, broke loose upon impact and crushed him. Another claims that he was dead before the crash, killed by a twenty-millimeter shot from German anti-aircraft guns as the gliders came over the coast.

Murphy's safety belt held the upper part of his body in the wreckage, but his badly broken legs protruded through the hole in the nose of the aircraft. His copilot was dead, and when he called out to the general's aide there was no answer. He was about to call out again when he heard a loud clanking sound. A German tank pulled up, just twenty yards away. Luckily, its crew apparently assumed no one could have survived the crash, and it rumbled on.

Murphy managed to slip out of the wreckage and was lying next to it when he was found by a medical technician who had landed in one of the other gliders. He tended to the pilot and the general's aide.

Most of the CG4-As in the D-Day mission were wrecked—not surprising, since crash landings were the rule rather than the exceptions as far as glider touchdowns were concerned. However, casualties were surprisingly light. General Pratt and five airborne troopers were killed, seventeen suffered severe injuries and seven were missing in action.

The original *Fighting Falcon*, flying in the number forty-five slot, wiped out its gear and skids in landing but stopped right on target. No one aboard was injured.

A half-century after D-Day, the story of Mission Chicago came to life again in a segment of 1998's award-winning motion picture, *Saving Private Ryan*—but not with complete regard for what actually happened. Though a CG4-A in the movie is not said to be the number one glider in the assault, the parallels can't be missed by persons who have seen the film and also are familiar with the facts concerning Murphy's aircraft and the actual airborne operation.

Saving Private Ryan opens with the D-Day invasion, then moves beyond the beaches and into enemy territory as Tom Hanks, as Captain John Miller, searches for Private James Ryan, whose three brothers had all been killed in combat. In the process, the searchers encounter a glider pilot and inspect the wreckage of his aircraft. Still in the shattered glider is the body of a brigadier general, identified by the pilot as deputy commander of the 101st Airborne Division.

The camera closes in to show the officer's helmet with its single star as the pilot complains that someone "had the great idea of welding a couple of steel plates onto our deck to keep the general safe from ground fire. Unfortunately, they forgot to tell me about it until we were just getting airborne. Well, it was like trying to fly a freight train. Gross overload."

In the actual D-Day glider assault, the only general aboard a 101st Airborne glider and the only general killed in a glider was Brigadier General Pratt, who was in the aircraft piloted by Murphy. In *Saving Private Ryan*, the glider pilot walks about as he shows Captain Miller and his men the wreckage and continues the diatribe concerning the armor plating in the aircraft. But when glider number one crashed, both of Murphy's legs were broken and he was unable to stand up, let alone walk.

"The others, they landed ok," the pilot in the movie says, inferring his was the only aircraft with casualties. He then adds, "Twenty-two guys dead." Actually, there were only four aboard the number one glider, and only two of them were dead. Moreover, twenty-two deaths in the crash of a single CG4-A would not have been possible since the glider was capable of carrying only thirteen men in addition to the pilot and copilot.

Certainly, departures from fact are to be expected in a fictional work. However, producers of the film appear to have been a bit careless in killing more men than the glider could carry.

CHAPTER 13

Buying a Bomber

While Greenville students were going all out to sell enough war bonds to send a Wago CG4-A glider into action against Axis forces during World War II, teenagers at South High School in Grand Rapids dreamed of putting something in the air, too. What they had in mind was a bomber—a Boeing B-17 Flying Fortress.

Both groups were fantastically successful. At Greenville, the young folk raised $72,000, sufficient to provide four gliders rather than the one that had been their goal. At South, the students collected $375,000 in their "Bomber for Victory" drive—a lot more than was necessary to buy a bomber.

On April 6, 1943, a month before the *Fighting Falcon* was christened at Black Athletic Field in Greenville, South High's students celebrated with a parade from Garfield Park to the Kent County Airport to see what they had bought and bask in the adulation of their elders.

Two jeeps, carrying South High School Queen LaVonne Kronberg and the five members of her court, led the procession while the school's 110-piece marching band strutted behind, providing the exciting sight and sound needed for the celebration.

At the airport, according to the *Grand Rapids Herald*, "the big bomber thundered across the field and pulled up before the speakers' stand, her heavy guns sheathed but nonetheless pictures of lethal efficiency. And when the South High School Band broke into the Army Air Corps song there was not a person in the audience who doubted that, with such ships as this, the fate of the Axis was sealed."

A huge crowd and the South High School Band welcomed a B-17 Flying Fortress bomber at Kent County Airport on April 6, 1943. In their "Bomber for Victory" campaign, students at the Grand Rapids school raised $375,000, much more than enough to pay for the plane. *Courtesy of Grand Rapids History and Special Collections, Archives, Grand Rapids Public Library.*

The plane—on which had been painted the school's Trojan emblem and its name, the *Spirit of South High*—was the first Flying Fortress ever seen in Grand Rapids, according to airport manager Thomas Walsh.

Among several speakers at the airport were Governor Harry F. Kelly; Grand Rapids Mayor George W. Welsh; Lieutenant Jack Goebel, a South alumnus who had been decorated for his service as a pilot in North Africa; and Henry Mulder, South faculty member in charge of the campaign. Appreciation was expressed to student leaders of the effort—Arthur Blackport and Melvin Hartger, who suggested the fundraising effort, and David Dutcher and Grace Moyer, who served as co-chairpersons.

Rather than break a bottle over the nose of the bomber, Queen Kronberg christened it by releasing a half dozen balloons of the school's colors, red and blue.

Aboard the aircraft when it arrived from Lockbourne Army Air Airfield in Columbus, Ohio, was Colonel A.C. Foulk, commander of the air base, and other officers. But there was one buck private on the plane, too—Walter J. Frydryck, who was stationed at the Ohio airfield. He and his wife, whose home was on Emerald Avenue, had not seen one another for two months. The plane, with its load of officers, went back to Columbus that afternoon, but Colonel Foulk gave the private permission to stay for an extra day.

Less than three weeks after the Japanese attack on Pearl Harbor and entry of the United States into World War II, sixteen-year-old South High freshman Charles "Buddy" Brott left his studies to join the U.S. Army Air Corps. Later, as a staff sergeant and crew chief at an air base in Italy, he was assigned to a new plane and went to check it out. It was the *Spirit of South High*!

Earlier, Brott had been offered an opportunity to apply for flight training, but he turned it down. It would have required showing a birth certificate, he explained, and he had fudged his age, of course, when he enlisted.

So he remained a mechanic—and a good one. His mother received a letter from Lieutenant Lloyd Babcock, pilot of one of the planes for which Brott had provided service. The message, written after the officer had completed ninety-four combat missions and returned to his home in California, said, "I wanted to tell you how much I enjoyed having your son with me. He has been a great help to me and is one of the most well-liked men at the base."

Brott, too, wrote a letter—to South High Principal Sherman Coryell—asking if it would be possible for him to complete his high school studies when he returned from service.

CHAPTER 14

When Whirlybirds First Flew

Few in Grand Rapids knew anything about helicopters, and none had ever seen one—not even the workers at a local refrigerator company who had been building major parts of the strange new aircraft for use in World War II operations. But then, during a sunny Saturday afternoon—May 26, 1945—three of these strange new contraptions appeared as specks on the eastern horizon and gradually grew as they approached the old Kent County Airport.

Though combat in Germany had ended, battles were still raging against the Japanese in the Pacific that day as hundreds crowded the apron in front of airline hangars at Grand Rapids. Most were employees of Nash-Kelvinator's Grand Rapids plant, which actually was on the Wyoming township side of Clyde Park Avenue, the border between the two municipalities. The parts manufactured by these men and women had been shipped to Nash-Kelvinator's Detroit complex for assembly and flight-testing.

And now they were going to see for the first time the finished product their contributions to the war effort had made possible. Gradually, the three amazing machines soared closer and closer to the airfield. Finally, they halted—while still in midair—and then slowly descended to the apron. Each of the unusual aircraft had two propellers, neither one in the customary up-front position. A huge one, on top, pointed straight up. The other, at the tail, was aimed sideways.

After they had slowly settled to the ground, some Nash-Kelvinator officials were lifted briefly a few feet into the air before the choppers flew off again.

Most others in the crowd just stood in awe, amazed that aircraft could do the kinds of things they were seeing.

During World War II, Nash-Kelvinator produced more than half the helicopters delivered to Allied military forces. But that wasn't its only contribution to the war effort. The company also was the largest wartime manufacturer of Hamilton Standard propellers that were used on bombers such as America's B-17 Flying Fortress, B-24 Liberator and B-25 Mitchell, as well as Britain's Avro Lancaster and De Havilland Mosquito. It also made governors for propeller mechanisms of Boeing, Consolidated North American and Martin bombers and for the navy's Consolidated PBY Catalina patrol bombers.

However, during the last stages of the war, production of parts for Sikorsky R-6 helicopters was the major project for the Grand Rapids industrial complex, which had been built in 1907 and for many years was the largest refrigerator factory in the world.

As it was about to begin production of the new aircraft, the company described the undertaking in a December 1943 magazine advertisement:

> *We are readying our production lines to build Sikorsky helicopters for the Army Air Forces. When and where and how the Army will use this new marvel of the air, which can rise vertically, hover motionless, fly forward or backward, is a military secret. But this can be told—this newest aerial marvel of the United Nations will be built only by Nash-Kelvinator and its designers, the Sikorsky Division of United Aircraft Corporation.*

In its report on the arrival of the trio of choppers at Kent County Airport in 1945, the *Grand Rapids Press* enlightened its readers with a definition of the amazing new contraption: "The helicopter is a versatile craft, capable of flying a hundred miles an hour and being able to move straight up or down, forward or backward."

Beneath a headline that proclaimed, "Egg-beaters swarm over GR Airport," *the Grand Rapids Herald* said, "You'd have thought they were three giant hummingbirds."

Citizens of Grand Rapids weren't the only ones at this time who knew little about helicopters. Although inventors had been trying for centuries to develop an aircraft that could mimic the movements of hummingbirds, they were constantly frustrated. Workable rotary-wing aircraft weren't produced anywhere in the world before the 1930s.

Leonardo da Vinci designed and tested experimental models in the 1400s, but without success. Thomas Alva Edison fashioned guncotton-powered helicopter models on this side of the ocean in the 1880s, but he gave up when an explosion singed him and severely burned an assistant.

Early in the twentieth century, Frenchmen Louis Charles Bregeut and Paul Cornu designed helicopters that were able to get into the air—but only a few feet above the ground. During the 1920s, Spain's Juan de la Cierva developed the autogiro, a peculiar cross between fixed-wing and rotary-wing aircraft. With the overhead rotors of future helicopters and the up-front propellers of airplanes, they could ascend and descend steeply, but not vertically. They couldn't hover unless they were headed into a stiff wind.

Nevertheless, it was Europeans who produced the first really practical helicopters. By 1935, Breguet designed what many consider to be the first completely successful helicopter. Eventually, it could reach a speed of seventy-five miles an hour and an altitude of 518 feet. It could remain aloft for more than an hour and could hover over one spot for ten minutes. But it was accident-prone and crashed several times.

About the same time, Heinrich Focke of Germany tested his FA-61 helicopter, which proved to be safer and more maneuverable. It looked like an autogiro because it kept the propeller up front, but that was just for cooling the craft's radial engine. Twin rotors, mounted on outriggers at each side of the fuselage, provided the propulsion.

To maximize the FA-61's propaganda value, the German government in February 1938 had twenty-five-year-old female pilot Hanna Reitsch fly the helicopter around the inside of the enclosed Deutschlandhalle sports stadium in Berlin for fourteen consecutive nights.

Anton Flettner also made progress in helicopter development for the Germans, and by 1942 two dozen of his FI-282s were in service. A thousand more were ordered for the Nazi military during World War II, but Allied bombing attacks kept them from being produced.

Meanwhile, on this side of the Atlantic, Russian émigré Igor Sikorsky matched the Europeans stride for stride, and his efforts were watched closely by U.S. military officials. After he came to America in 1923, he founded Sikorsky Aero Engineering Corporation. After six years, he was bought out and his company became a division of United Aircraft. Though he spent most of his time on production of seaplanes, he worked on helicopter design in his spare time.

Though the Depression forced United Aircraft to close its Sikorsky Division, it permitted Sikorsky to head a team to develop a helicopter. He succeeded on September 14, 1939, when his Vought-Sikorsky-300, though tethered, managed to get off the ground. It wasn't pretty. There wasn't a

The first time Nash-Kelvinator employees saw the strange new aircraft for which they'd been building the major parts was on May 26, 1945. That day three of them, the first helicopters ever seen at Grand Rapids, flew from Detroit where they had been assembled and tested. Nash-Kelvinator produced more than half the helicopters used by Allied forces during World War II. *Given to author by Grand Rapids Press photographer Earl Spielmacher.*

fuselage or cockpit—just a naked framework with a single three-bladed main rotor, an anti-torque tail rotor, a sixty-five-horsepower engine and an exposed pilot's seat. But it worked.

Besides, it was the first workable helicopter that didn't need two rotors revolving in opposite directions to eliminate torque. He solved the problem with the tail rotor that provided thrust in the direction opposite to that of the torque. There were two serious crashes of the aircraft, but with patience and persistence, Sikorsky worked out the problems, and by 1941, he had the technology to build a production machine.

That year United Aircraft's Vought-Sikorsky Division signed a contract with the U.S. Army Air Force to develop the VS-316A, later designated the XR-4. It had a steel framework, canvas-covered except the rear end of the fuselage, and its cabin had side-by-side seating with dual controls for a two-man crew.

After the R-4 prototype of the aircraft made a test flight at Stratford, Connecticut, in January 1942, it was flown to Wright Field at Dayton, Ohio. While pilot Les Morris flew the helicopter, an automobile with a big yellow dot painted on the roof followed below, carrying an engineer and a mechanic. Whenever red lights forced the car to stop, Morris would astonish other motorists by halting the aircraft in midair and hovering over the auto. At refueling stops, he'd surprise ground crews standing in front of hangars by speeding toward them and then, when they scrambled for cover, he'd halt and hover for a moment before gently settling to the ground just feet from the hangar.

Word about the amazing flight was kept confidential for nearly a year. Then, in March 1943, *Newsweek* reported the accomplishment and described the new airship: "It rises and descends vertically, without running space. It flies forward or backward. It shies to either side, can bounce on the air, spin like a top on its vertical axis, or hover motionless over a definite spot." The magazine noted that Sikorsky, who piloted the aircraft on the last leg of the trip, departed from usual procedure in getting landing approval. He hovered next to the control tower and called out, "This is Igor Sikorski. It is ok to land?"

Among the welcomers at Dayton was Orville Wright. He was asked several times if he'd like to go up in the R-4, but he politely refused every time.

Vought-Sikorsky produced a later version of the helicopter, the R-5, before it gave birth to the R-6, a streamlined version of the R-4 with the same rotor and transmission, but improved pilot visibility and a metal fuselage. Extensive use of magnesium and casting alloys made the craft lighter than the R-4 without sacrificing structural integrity.

A joint army-navy contract for five XR-6A prototypes of the aircraft was signed on April 30, 1943, and the first flight of one was made the following October. In March 1944, one of the XR-6As with litter capsules for carrying wounded flew to Washington, D.C., where military officials checked its capability. The surgeon general insisted that he and some of his staff be permitted to try out the litters, so several flights were made with a passenger in the copilot's seat and in each of the two litters. Despite the overload, the tests were successful.

A day later, the chopper was flown to Wright Field at Dayton by pilot Frank Gregory and engineer Ralph Alex, but they were dangerously low on fuel and decided to land at Patterson Field, a few miles away. When they put the aircraft down near a large plane, they were immediately surrounded by military police. "The big airplane turned out to be the first B-29 delivered to the Army Air Forces," Alex recalled. "The field had been closed for this event, and it took some frantic explanations before we were allowed to refuel and fly to Wright Field."

At the time the army ordered twenty-six YR-6A production models later that year, Vought-Sikorsky was under pressure to step up production of its F4U Corsair fighter planes for the navy and marine corps. So, to avoid pulling skilled personnel from the gull-winged fighter project, United Aircraft rejected the helicopter contract but agreed to license production of the YR-6As to the Kelvinator Division of Nash-Kelvinator Corporation.

Production arrangements were reported later by Grand Rapids newspapers—at the time of the flight of the three R-6s to the city in May 1945. The *Grand Rapids Herald* quoted O.L. Currier, manager of the Grand Rapids factory, as saying it "makes the entire ship with exception of the motor." The *Grand Rapids Press* version added a few more parts made elsewhere: "The entire helicopter except the engine, rotor blades, and equipment such as radio is made in the Grand Rapids plant. The cabin is assembled in one section and the tailcone in another and are shipped to Detroit where the helicopter is assembled and given test flights."

To keep production lines at Grand Rapids rolling when the supply of minor parts such as fasteners ran out, Kelvinator employees got substitutes at local hardware stores. Two were located conveniently—Jelsema's Hardware, directly across Clyde Park Avenue from the plant's main entrance, and Groen's Hardware, adjacent to the factory at the corner of Clyde Park and Grandville Avenues. The substitution policy prompted some at Vought-Sikorsky to refer to the Kelvinator-made aircraft as "Kelvicopters" and "Refrigerotors."

An unidentified helicopter pilot points out flight instruments to Thomas Walsh, Kent County Airport manager, (seated in the aircraft) and O. L. Currier, manager of the Grand Rapids Division of Nash-Kelvinator Corporation. *Given to author by* Grand Rapids Press *photographer Earl Spielmacher.*

But Vought-Sikorsky officials were impressed by Kelvinator's speed in turning out the helicopters. "The production tooling of most of the components was a wonder to behold," one said, "especially for us in the aircraft industry." And it wasn't just the quality. The quantities were exceptional, too. Many parts were made at twice the monthly rate required by the contract.

Completion of the twenty-six preproduction models led to a larger order for Nash-Kelvinator, and during 1944–45, the company manufactured 193 of them.

Some R-6s had capsules on each side of the fuselage so they could carry litters for medical evacuation, and some had floats for operation from water. A few, with racks installed for bombs and depth charges, underwent tests to determine whether they would be effective in assaults against ground forces, ships and submarines.

Several of the R-6s made by Kelvinator were used for emergency rescue operations in the China-Burma-India Theater of Operations during 1945, recovering several Allied pilots at altitudes as high as eight thousand feet. Some were also used for medical evacuations, but their principal use during World War II was in observation and liaison. In addition to the helicopters for the U.S. Army Air Corps, some went to the navy and the Coast Guard and others were sent to Great Britain for use by the Royal Navy and Royal Air Force.

In the waning days of the war, an R-6 was sent on a scientific mission to explore what was described as "the first new volcano to be born in the time of man." It had erupted in a farmer's field near Paricutan, Mexico. The field was 7,000 feet above sea level, and the cone of the 1,800-foot-high volcano was a mile in diameter at the base. The R-6 enabled scientists to examine the volcano at close range and even descend into the crater when it was not expected to erupt.

Before leaving Mexico, the R-6 encountered strong winds while flying over mountains and rapidly lost altitude. When the helicopter, with Ralph Alex and pilot Roy Beer aboard, landed in a small clearing, the landing gear broke, the engine tore loose and the main blades came down and severed the tail cone. Back in the United States, it was reported that Alex and Beer were dead.

However, when the storm subsided, the airmen—very much alive—found themselves surrounded by Tarascan Indians armed with rifles. The Indians told residents of a nearby village that the Americans would be released if an appropriate ransom were paid. Within a few hours, rescuers, who apparently had started out when the fliers were presumed dead, arrived. With them were two extra, unsaddled horses, for bringing back the corpses. Alex and Beer rode them thirty miles down the mountain on makeshift saddles fashioned from blankets. They went to Mexico City by jeep the next day and then to the United States by commercial airline.

Helicopters stopped rolling off Grand Rapids assembly lines almost immediately after the Japanese surrender in August 1945. All the choppers made in the United States for the Allies during World War II were Sikorski models—128 R-4s, 64 R-5s and 291 R-6s, a total of 412 aircraft. The 219 R-6s manufactured by Nash-Kelvinator in Grand Rapids and Detroit accounted for more than half of these machines.

Besides the helicopters that were delivered to military forces, Nash-Kelvinator produced 205 more before the war ended. They were accepted by the army and shipped to Randolph Field in Texas, where they were stored in sheds. Eventually, they were scrapped when rust and deterioration made them unusable.

Although helicopters didn't play a dramatic role in World War II, the Sikorsky models proved these aircraft could complete useful wartime missions. During the Korean War a few years later, choppers were familiar sights in search-rescue and medical evacuation roles. In Vietnam during the 1960s and '70s, they transported troops and assaulted enemy positions, bringing about a radical change in the ways wars were fought. In more recent conflicts, they carried out assaults against enemy vehicles and troops and ferried American soldiers deep into enemy territory.

And, in 2012, it was Black Hawk helicopters that transported Navy SEALs into Osama bin Laden's Pakistan compound, where they eliminated him in retribution for the September 11, 2001, attacks on the Twin Towers of the World Trade Center complex in New York City and the Pentagon in Arlington, Virginia.

More important, helicopters have contributed greatly to a better life for many and have had significant roles in a wide variety of everyday functions such as observation and control of highway traffic, law enforcement, firefighting, news gathering, emergency medical response, crop-dusting, power line patrols and placement of heavy equipment atop buildings.

On that sunny Saturday in May 1945, few in the crowd at Grand Rapids dreamed the strange craft hovering above them would end up doing things like that.

CHAPTER 15

All from a Mess in the Icebox

The large Grand Rapids industrial complex, where major parts for most of the helicopters used by Allied forces during World War II were manufactured, has disappeared. Built by Charles H. Leonard at the western edge of the city, it began producing appliances for his Grand Rapids Refrigerator Company in the early 1900s.

Leonard had manufactured refrigerators earlier at several other locations after beginning on the second floor of his father's store in downtown Grand Rapids. The older Leonard, Herman, came to Michigan from Parma, New York, in 1842. He worked two years as landlord of the Eagle Hotel before opening a grocery store. Eventually the groceries were replaced by household goods, and Charles and his brothers, Frank and Fred, joined the business, which became H. Leonard and Sons, importers and jobbers of crockery, china and glassware.

It was a messy meltdown that led Charles into appliance manufacturing. Soon after his marriage, he had purchased an Indiana-made icebox, and the family's maid carelessly placed a hot pail of lard atop the block of ice in the cooling compartment of the refrigerator, then forgot it. When the ice started to melt, the pail tipped, and the lard spilled throughout the ice chamber and down the wastewater pipe, blocking it completely. As Charles struggled to clean up the mess, he decided he could build a better icebox.

The result was the Leonard Cleanable Refrigerator, and soon he and Frank were building and selling them at the family store. In the mid-1880s, the refrigerator operations, which had been just one facet of the Leonards'

This huge Nash-Kelvinator complex on Clyde Park Avenue was where principal parts for helicopters were produced during World War II. The main building was constructed in 1907 and, for many years, was the world's largest refrigerator factory.

business, became known as Grand Rapids Refrigerator Company. It was incorporated under that name in 1904. A few years later, twenty-six acres were purchased on the west side of Clyde Park Avenue and construction of the big new factory began. In 1907, Charles built what was described by the *Grand Rapids Furniture Record* of November 1908 as "the immense new plant of the Grand Rapids Refrigerator Company. For the purpose intended, this is the largest and most complete plant in the world." The complex eventually would employ more workers than were on the payroll of any other West Michigan company.

At the beginning, the new factory turned out only ice-cooled refrigerators, but within a few years Leonard formed an alliance with Electro-Automatic Refrigerating Company of Detroit, soon renamed the Kelvinator Company. In 1918, the Grand Rapids firm made Kelvinator's first cabinets, designed specifically for electric refrigeration. In 1926, the company's name was changed to Leonard Refrigerator Company, and it was acquired by Kelvinator.

Kelvinator joined with Nash Motors in 1937 to form Nash-Kelvinator Corporation. Then, in 1954, the largest merger in the automotive industry to date impacted Grand Rapids when Nash-Kelvinator merged with Hudson Motor Car Company to form American Motors Corporation. At that time, there were eighty-six buildings at the large industrial complex, which produced not only refrigerators but also electric ranges, washing machines, driers, freezers and ice cream cabinets.

Though final assembly of the Sikorsky R-6 helicopters made by Nash-Kelvinator—with parts shipped from Grand Rapids—was completed in Detroit, the procedure for refrigerator production throughout most of Kelvinator's history had parts moving in the opposite direction. Trucks then carried refrigerator systems and compressors made at the Detroit plant to the Grand Rapids factory, which produced the cabinets and did the final assembly. The 165-mile route was highway U.S. 16, which Kelvinator considered its "asphalt conveyor."

In 1968, the Kelvinator facilities in Grand Rapids were sold to White Consolidated Industries, and in 1977, the last refrigerator to be made in Grand Rapids rolled off the assembly line. A.B. Electrolux of Sweden bought White Consolidated in 1986, and a year later the plant closed when the company moved stove production to plants in Ohio and Tennessee.

Delta Properties purchased the Clyde Park Avenue complex in 1988 and leased portions of the main building and subsidiary structures to smaller concerns. In 1996, fire destroyed production facilities of several of these companies, and demolition of the eighty-five-year-old factory began. Fires broke out in the building again in February and March of 1997 as razing of the structure continued.

Sadly, Leonard's pride and joy now lives on only in the memories of a dwindling number of workers who spent much of their lives within its walls. But what had started out to darken a day in the Leonard kitchen more than a century earlier proved to bring good fortune for many years to the Leonards—and to all of the Grand Rapids area.

CHAPTER 16

All-out for the Allies

The helicopters made by Nash-Kelvinator and the gliders produced by Grand Rapids Industries weren't the city's only contributions to the military might of Allied forces during World War II. Scores of the city's manufacturing companies and their thousands of workers, men and women alike, forged the tools that were needed to preserve freedom. And their efforts weren't something new. They had done the same during World War I.

While both wars raged, consortia of Grand Rapids manufacturers formed and multiplied the contributions that member companies could make. The peacetime production of most of them had created some of the world's best furniture, but their wartime efforts turned out materiel needed by military forces of the Allies.

More than a dozen manufacturers combined their efforts during World War I after forming a consortium known as the Grand Rapids Airplane Company. That approach was used again during World War II when several member companies united to create Grand Rapids Industries.

Grand Rapids Airplane Company's World War I efforts for the Allies resulted in production of 365 huge Handley-Page 0/400 biplane bombers. Though Handley-Page was a British corporation, many of the bombers were built in the United States.

The planes, with a hundred-foot wingspread and a fuselage that was more than sixty-two feet long, were the largest aircraft that had been built in Britain up to that time and were among the biggest in the world. Those made in Grand Rapids were shipped unassembled to stations in Britain

Handley-Page bombers, like this one, were the largest planes of their kind during World War I. A consortium of furniture manufacturers, Grand Rapids Airplane Company, made 365 of them. However, the war ended before any of the huge planes from the Furniture City could get into action in Europe.

and the United States. The only parts not made in Grand Rapids were the 360-horsepower Rolls-Royce engines.

Principal components of the aircraft were wood and fabric. About 98 percent of the lumber used at Grand Rapids was spruce, which was dried in thirty-eight kilns with a capacity of 300,000 feet per week.

The Handley-Page 0/400s had an exceptionally heavy bomb load for a World War I plane, usually carrying sixteen 112-pound or eight 250-pound bombs inside with additional ones on external racks. Occasionally, the bombers carried a single 1,650-pound bomb. Twin Lewis machine guns were mounted in the plane's two cockpits, one at the nose and another atop the fuselage facing rear, with a third set at the floor of the fuselage. The pilot and copilot were in the nose cockpit.

The big bombers had a maximum speed of 97 miles per hour and a range of 700 miles. Their wings could be folded back for hangar storage.

Production of the 0/400s began late in the war, and none of those made in Grand Rapids saw action overseas. Nevertheless, an article in the June

1919 *Furniture Manufacturer and Artisan* magazine contended the aircraft made in Grand Rapids helped to bring the war to an end:

> *Yet those gigantic machines...undoubtedly contributed to that full measure of retribution about to be precipitated upon the Hun, which led his shrinking autocrats to plead for leniency and sign the armistice on November 11, 1918. For it is conceded by those familiar with America's preparation for the anticipated campaign of 1919, that Handley-Page airplanes made in Grand Rapids formed an important part of that huge quantity of war materials being produced in this country—the menace of which did more to end the war than any exhaustion of Germany's military strength, fancied or real. Thus, Grand Rapids, through the conscientious application of its industrial resources and manufacturing ideals to a patriotic end, served to save the lives of some 200,000 American doughboys who might have been sacrificed had the war continued.*

Member companies of the consortium were: Berkey and Gay Furniture, Century Furniture, Grand Rapids Chair, Grand Rapids Furniture, Grand Rapids Show Case, Imperial Furniture, Johnson Furniture, Luce Furniture, Macey, Royal Furniture, Phoenix Furniture, Sligh Furniture, Stickley Brothers, John Widdicomb and Wilmarth Show Case.

When the war ended, 110 of the aircraft made in Grand Rapids were at an assembly station in Oldham, England, and 200 were ready to be shipped.

Also contributing to the Allied arsenal during World War I was a smaller company, Michigan Aircraft, which evolved from the 1916 flying boat project at Reeds Lake. Tony Stadlman and Bert Kenyon, who were involved in that venture, were among about ten Michigan Aircraft staff members in 1917. Their base of operations then was in what had been the Pastime Vaudette, a vaudeville theater on Wealthy Street. Today, it's the Wealthy Theater.

The company was incorporated in June 1917 and, by autumn, had generated considerable enthusiasm, especially among local journalists. The *Grand Rapids Press* reported on October 8:

> *In the modest little plant of the Michigan Aircraft Company at 1130 Wealthy Street, SE, two beautiful biplanes are nearing completion, and experts in aviation and airplane design and construction are unanimous in their conviction that these machines are among the finest ever turned out in America...*
>
> *The big flying boat with its superstreamlined body and forty-five-foot wing spread is built to specifications outlined by the government but,*

in working out his body design and rib sections of the planes, designer Anthony Stadlman has gone a step ahead, according to the British and American aviation experts who have been sent here to inspect the work of the local plant.

Two boats already have been built and proved stable and speedy in a summer's flying along the east shore of Lake Michigan. In these, the ideas of the designer were proved out and now the flying company is building a flying boat and military tractor to meet the requirements of the United States Army and Navy.

The planes also featured a dual control system that had been developed by Kenyon. When the aircraft would be used for training pilots, the instructor could disengage the student's controls, if necessary, and take over. In pointing out the need for such a system, the newspaper noted that "Fish" Hassell had recently been instructing a student who panicked and locked the controls in a grip so strong that Hassell "was forced to break the man's wrist to gain control of the falling plane."

In a February 17, 1918 story, the *Grand Rapids Herald* said that one of Michigan Aviation Company's planes would be on display the next day:

Visitors at the ninth annual Automobile Show, which opens tomorrow in the Klingman Building under the Auspices of the Grand Rapids Automobile Association, will have their first real opportunity to see the latest product of Grand Rapids only hydro-aeroplane factory, which before many weeks pass will undoubtedly be contracted for extensive use by the Navy Department of the United States.

An appealing feature of the plane, the *Herald* said, was the seating arrangement—one occupant sitting directly in front of the other, rather than side by side as in earlier aircraft. This, according to the paper, "narrows the body of the plane and greatly lessens the wind resistance, resulting in greater speed." In reference to the arrangement, the report claimed the plane "is the only machine having it in the country."

Despite the enthusiasm of the newsmen, however, Michigan Aviation Company soon faded from the scene; and in the 1920s, the building again became a theater.

A major contributor to the cause of the Allies in both World Wars was Haskelite Manufacturing Corporation, which opened its Grand Rapids plant in April 1918. It specialized in products made from molded plywood sheets—three or more layers of veneer that were bonded with Henry L. Haskell's waterproof glue. Before the World War I armistice was signed in November, Haskelite had about four hundred employees and was operating twenty-four hours a day.

Among the war materiel produced by the corporation were fuselages and propellers for aircraft, pontoons for hydroplanes and gunstocks.

In 1918, fuselages for two models of Curtiss airplanes—the fastest and most heavily armed fighter planes of their day—were manufactured by Haskelite. The 18-B Hornet was a biplane, and the 18-T Wasp was a triplane. The 18-T soon set several records: world speed record of 163.1 miles per hour with a load of 1,067 pounds on August 19, 1918; American altitude record of 30,100 feet on July 25, 1919; and world altitude record of 34,610 feet on September 18, 1919.

The *Herald* described the 18-T and the tenacity of Haskelite products in a December 1918 article:

> *Navy officials have adopted a new type of triplane which they will use exclusively for the twenty-one coastal air stations that are to be established immediately. The new type of triplane has the world's record for speed of this type of craft in tests, making a record of 163 miles per hour... The fuselage of this record breaking aircraft was manufactured right here in Grand Rapids by the Haskelite plant. It is known as the "Whistling Benny," and is made of four molded skins put together on frame work. The local plant turned it out with no angles or sharp corners which would hinder its speed.*
>
> *One little incident showing the durability of Haskelite was heard a short time ago from an officer of the British Navy, who was visiting in this country. He told of an airplane, built largely of Haskelite, which was sunk in British waters and a week later raised. He stated that after two days, repairs on it and some new parts in the machinery, it sailed away in the air again on the fourth day.*

During World War I, Haskelite produced more than five million square feet of plywood for construction of British, French and U.S. warplanes. After the war, it also furnished plywood components for Charles Lindbergh's *Spirit of St. Louis.*

Among Haskelite's early contributions to the Allied cause in World War II were plywood parts for Britain's De Havilland Mosquito fighter bombers, one of the few combat aircraft constructed almost entirely of wood and nicknamed the "Wooden Wonder."

In a story entitled "The Furniture City Joins the Air War," the April 1943 edition of *Aero Digest* told its readers that Haskelite "once turned out plywood for trains, ships, stores, and buses, but now supplies most of its output to aviation. Haskelite plywood goes into the manufacture of trainers, gliders, bombers, and transports."

Regarding the war efforts of Furniture City industries, the magazine said:

> *When you think of airplanes, you don't think of Grand Rapids. Yet the list of materials and parts it is supplying to America's Number One industry is growing in both scope and volume. Grand Rapids furnishes America with wings, fuselages, floors and control surfaces for gliders, trainers, and bombers; seats for pilots, vital parts of bomb and aerial torpedoes to drop on enemy targets; parachutes to bail out with; refueling equipment for North Africa and the Solomons; propeller blades; machine tools for airplane makers; plywood for a host of purposes; dopes, sealers, and finishes for surfaces; instruments to guide the ships; dollies and conveyors for factories and maintenance; metal belts for aircraft armament; and ammunition to put into the belts. The list is endless.*
>
> *It takes a Cook's grand tour of the environs to understand how this pleasant home-owning city of 175,000 persons is making itself indispensable to the war in the air. The job of conversion was begun long before Pearl Harbor by a number of far-sighted concerns. It received an impetus with the glider program; another boost when the use of wood in aircraft was encouraged to save critical materials.*

Haskelite was one of several companies in a consortium known as Grand Rapids Industries, which provided components for Waco CG-4A gliders made at Gibson Refrigerator Company in Greenville and at Cessna Aircraft Company in Wichita, Kansas. Grand Rapids Industries also made a few gliders itself.

Another member of the consortium, American Seating Company, produced wings for training planes and pilot's seats made of plywood. The factory of Imperial Furniture Company was the site of final assembly for wings and other large parts of gliders produced by other Grand Rapids Industries members.

Among other companies contributing to Grand Rapids Industries efforts were: Brower Furniture, William A. Berkey Furniture, Grand Rapids Chair, Hekman Furniture, Johnson Furniture, Kindel Furniture, Mueller Furniture, Murray Furniture, Nichols & Cox Lumber, Valley City Furniture,

Before World War II, the manufacturing skills of these and other Grand Rapids workers turned out furniture, appliances and other consumer goods. Then, to help the Allied cause during the war, they used those same skills to produce a wide variety of parts for aircraft of all kinds. *Courtesy of Grand Rapids History and Special Collections, Archives, Grand Rapids Public Library.*

Widdicomb Furniture, John Widdicomb Company, Williams-Kemp Furniture and Baker Furniture of Holland.

Other plants, not affiliated with Grand Rapids Industries, also provided a wide variety of equipment for the Allies. Hayes Manufacturing Corporation made dive bomber wing panels, parachutes, parts for torpedoes and bomb tailfins. Grand Rapids Varnish Company furnished the aviation industry with enamels, dopes, thinners, sealers and aircraft motor finishes.

Berkey and Gay Furniture Company, which had been in business for more than ninety years, devoted a hundred percent of its efforts to aviation, making plywood fuselages and stabilizers for North American Aviation's T-6 Texan trainers, the aircraft in which most of World War II's Allied pilots learned to fly. Molded plywood sections from Haskelite were used by Berkey and Gay to make the parts. Of the Berkey and Gay workforce, 45 percent were women.

Winters and Crampton, which previously had manufactured hardware for refrigerators and stoves, produced wing-gun ammunition boxes, parts for aircraft engines, struts for landing gears and radio capacitors.

Tannewitz Works remained in its customary field, making band saws. It furnished aircraft manufacturers with die saws, variable speed band saws and high-speed sheet metal saws. Carter Products Company, which produced band saw wheels, began providing them for aircraft manufacturers. Blackmer Pump Company didn't have to convert for aviation production either. Since it had been producing fuel pumps for airlines throughout the world, the war brought only an expansion of its business.

Rapids-Standard Company also kept producing the same product that it had during peacetime—conveyors. But it also turned out propeller dollies, plastic wheels for glider tail assemblies and materials handling equipment for airplane manufacturers.

Grand Rapids Store Equipment Company, then said to be the largest business of its kind in the world, switched from making things like counters and display equipment to ailerons for Vought F4U Corsair fighter planes and toolboxes for Packard Merlin aircraft engines. Allen Calculators switched from adding machines to aircraft bank-and-turn indicators.

Besides Sikorsky R-6 helicopters, Nash-Kelvinator Corporation produced parts for other aircraft for the Allies. It started out making parts for Consolidated Catalina flying boats, but the work was discontinued soon after it was begun. Then it produced Hamilton-Standard hydromatic propellers.

Though attempts in Grand Rapids to arm the Allies during World War I came too late to make a big difference, the efforts of workers at that time matched those of the greater number of men and women who contributed to America's Arsenal of Democracy during World War II. During both wars, Grand Rapids craftsmen—who had been building tables and chairs, refrigerators and hardware—helped pave the road to victory.

CHAPTER 17

Flying to Freedom

Through the years, airplanes have brought millions of passengers to Grand Rapids. Some came to handle business affairs. Some wanted to gather with family and friends. Some sought relaxation along the shore of nearby Lake Michigan.

And some came to find freedom and to rebuild shattered lives.

That started happening soon after World War II ended in Europe, bringing about the largest population movements in the continent's history. Peace had returned, but European countries were in turmoil. Thousands of persons had been displaced during the war. Germans had imprisoned citizens of occupied countries, and Jews from their own, in concentration camps. Thousands of others were forced to move to distant factories and produce war materiel for the Nazis.

Now released, and with nowhere to go, the survivors dreamed of a better life in a better place—a place free from fear, hunger and hatred. For some of the most fortunate, it was found in West Michigan.

Earlier immigrants had crossed the ocean on sailing ships and steamers, the voyages often taking more than a month. Then they faced further travel in a river craft or wagon—or perhaps a walk of hundreds of miles. When railroad tracks reached Grand Rapids in the late 1850s, traveling was easier, and the arrival of buses in the twentieth century provided another option.

However, it wasn't until the middle of the 1900s that airplanes began bringing Europeans to Kent County Airport and their new homes nearby.

Most of them had never flown before. So the flight often was a strange mixture of stressful anxiety and eager anticipation.

Some of the Europeans who sought refuge in America had relatives who had come to the Grand Rapids area many years before. Now, many of those persons and their descendants reached out to make a new start in a new land possible for their kinfolk—and sometimes even for strangers.

That's the kind of thing that opened the door for Meindert Vander Iest and his wife, Blyke, who came from the Netherlands in August 1948 with their daughters, Sapke, eight; Sietske, six; Neetje, four; and Antonia, one. Dutch immigrants had been coming to West Michigan for a century, and many of their descendants lived in and near Grand Rapids. Two of them were the De Witt brothers, Jack and Dick, who owned the Zeeland Hatchery. Meindert was a poultryman, and they hired him to assist in their operations.

Meindert had gotten into the poultry business in Europe at the worst of times—1939. World War II broke out when Germany invaded Poland on September 1 of that year. Then Hitler's forces crossed the border into the Netherlands on May 10, 1940, and the Dutch surrendered four days later. Even after the Nazis were expelled by the Allies and the war ended in 1945, the situation in the Netherlands was not good.

"There was no chance for a man to get ahead," Meindert said. "And there was no chance for the children."

Most who came from Europe at that time still crossed the Atlantic in ships, but the Vander Iests learned that a wait of months would be necessary before passage on a ship could be obtained. So they came by plane and landed at Kent County Airport.

Today, of course, virtually all who seek a new chance in West Michigan come by air and touch down at Gerald R. Ford International Airport.

It was the end of another war that touched off one of the greatest influxes of newcomers to the Grand Rapids area. And it all started on an airplane.

The year was 1975, and on April 30, North Vietnamese forces captured Saigon and renamed it Ho Chi Minh City. The war in Vietnam was over, but many from South Vietnam now were refugees. In southern California on that day, a Grand Rapids pastor and his wife, Howard and Marybelle Schipper, were aboard a plane and ready to take off for home.

They had been in Orange City for a national church conference with Dr. Robert H. Schuller at the Crystal Cathedral. His advice to the church leaders who attended was to go back home and make a difference in their ministries. "Find a need, and fill it," he said.

As the Schippers waited for their plane to leave the terminal, they pondered what kind of need they might be able to fill. Seated just a few rows away were several Vietnamese children, survivors of a plane crash who were being escorted to Boston by Catholic nuns. As Reverend Schipper looked at the children, he realized they had left behind everything that was familiar. They, like all refugees, didn't have the option of going home. They had virtually nothing. "Here's a very large need," he said to his wife. "Let's fill it!"

Bringing refugees to Grand Rapids and helping them rebuild their lives is something we could do, they thought. Perhaps they could bring a planeload. They decided to try forming a consortium of churches to make that happen. They'd call the effort "Freedom Flight."

Back in Grand Rapids, the Schippers pursued the idea with members of their church and with leaders of other congregations in the city. Acquaintances Dr. William Vander Muelen and his wife, Wilma, were close friends of President Gerald R. Ford and had been invited to an upcoming State Department dinner at the White House. They offered to share the plan with the president and see what officials in Washington might do to help.

From Washington, Dr. Ver Meulen called the Schippers and said that those he approached liked the idea. "They want a telegram from you," he said. "But anything you ask for ought to be doubled, because the feds usually just cut things in half. So double whatever you think you're going to do."

Reverend Schipper sent off a telegram, telling about progress being made in formation of a consortium of fifty to a hundred churches and the group's hopes for resettling up to a hundred refugee families. A response arrived soon, expressing the State Department's gratitude for the offer of help and advising that it would contact an agency at Fort Chaffee, Arkansas, "to get in touch with you in making arrangements to send up to one hundred families to the Grand Rapids area." It didn't cut the number in half, as Dr. Vander Meulen had expected.

Fort Chaffee was the site where the Vietnamese were being processed for resettlement, and the State Department suggested the consortium contact the agency there to correlate efforts.

As planning proceeded, Grand Rapids Public Schools Superintendent Philip Runkel called a May 23 meeting of representatives from industry, labor, voluntary agencies and others who might be able to contribute to success of the resettlement effort. About a hundred persons were present, and they formed a sixteen-member Freedom Flight Task Force to create and coordinate programs that would meet their goals. Reverend Schipper was elected chairman of the task force.

Only three weeks had passed since the Schippers had determined that the need they'd try to fill was providing a better life for refugees. Now an ecumenical, community-wide group was proceeding to make their dream come true.

What had started as a committee became a task force, and eventually it would lead to establishment of Freedom Flight Refugee Center. Headed by the Schippers, it continued to assist refugees for more than two decades.

Before the end of May 1975, Reverend Schipper and other task force members made the first of several trips to Fort Chaffee, where they eventually interviewed 125 refugee families. The first four fugitives from Vietnam arrived at the airport in Grand Rapids during Memorial Day weekend. By the end of June, twelve families—forty individuals—had come to the city.

In July, the largest group of Vietnamese refugees to arrive at one time walked out of a plane at the airport in Grand Rapids and into the arms of new American friends and relatives who had preceded them. There were fifty-two of them, and it was one of the most exciting welcomes the city has ever seen.

"An excited scene of handshakes, hugs, and eager greetings unfolded," Reverend Schipper recalled, "bringing warmth to the battered souls of the newcomers and overcoming their initial feelings of uneasiness. Present amidst the hubbub was the Vietnamese group's first American citizen, a baby girl born just a few days earlier at Fort Chaffee. In a gesture of gratitude, her parents named her Marybelle after my wife."

President Ford, unable to be present, sent a telegram to Reverend Schipper:

Mrs. Ford and I wholeheartedly welcome the Vietnamese refugees who will be making their new home in Grand Rapids. We are deeply proud of the initiative and close cooperation shown by the area's churches and many fellow townsmen in making this effort possible. Your enthusiasm in sponsoring this worthwhile project reflects the basic philosophy of American life. It is a tribute to our national heritage. I hope that you will convey our warmest greetings to these newcomers. We join you in wishing them every happiness and a good life in our community.

And more kept coming. By the end of summer, Grand Rapids had opened its hearts to 231 refugees, and before the end of the year, 577 had been resettled in the city. There were then 101 families, exceeding the original estimate. And still they kept coming. By 1976, the total reached 797 individuals in 145 families.

Howard Schipper, shown here with a few of the thousands of Vietnamese children whose happiness he rekindled, wanted to bring one planeload of refugees to Grand Rapids. The efforts of him and his wife, Marybelle, to make that happen eventually resulted in establishment of an agency that helped more than 11,000 fugitives from tragedy in all parts of the world fly into Kent County Airport and rebuild their lives in West Michigan. *Courtesy of Grand Rapids History and Special Collections, Archives, Grand Rapids Public Library.*

The tide then slowed, and it appeared there'd be no more Vietnamese aboard planes landing at the airport in Grand Rapids. But that didn't last long. Only the first wave of refugees had fled. Now throngs were crowding onto flimsy boats and heading into the ocean in search of safety and freedom. Some of the crowded boats sank, and others were attacked by marauding pirates. As many as half of these refugees, the "boat people," perished.

Some estimated that as many as 400,000 survived and reached refugee camps in neighboring countries where conditions were hardly better. In America, Congress passed the Refugee Act of 1980, which reduced restrictions on Vietnamese immigration and opened the door for the "boat people" to be resettled in the United States.

At the same time, the United Nations High Commissioner for Refugees reached an agreement with Vietnam establishing an Orderly Departure Program (ODP) that permitted Vietnamese to leave the country for humanitarian reasons or reunification with relatives abroad.

When the Orderly Departure Program (ODP) opened a door permitting refugees still in Vietnam to join relatives in America, thousands of Vietnamese went to Kent County Airport, where they reached out to greet loved ones they thought they might never see again. *Courtesy of Grand Rapids History and Special Collections, Archives, Grand Rapids Public Library.*

Those developments led to more planes with refugees aboard taking off from Southeast Asia, and many of the journeys ended at the airport in Grand Rapids. Freedom Flight resettled more than a thousand from this wave of refugees by 1981.

Before the end of the decade, Congress passed the Amerasian Homecoming Act, which opened the door for children of American GI fathers and Vietnamese mothers to enter the United States through ODP. They could bring accompanying relatives—mother, siblings and stepfather, if there was one—with them.

In Vietnam, the Amerasians had suffered discrimination because their appearance was a reminder of a former enemy. But now, they became a hot commodity—a ticket to America! Immigration officials needed to be alert for false claims by Vietnamese youth who said they were Amerasian and by women who asserted that an Amerasian was their child.

Thousands of Amerasians and their Vietnamese kin soon arrived in the United States, and the lives of hundreds of them began to change as soon as they landed in Grand Rapids.

Refugees from Vietnam continued to come to the city through ODP, and after the horror inflicted by the communist Khmer Rouge on the people of Cambodia, hundreds of refugees from that country came to West Michigan with help from Freedom Flight Refugee Center.

The center continued to assist refugees until 1999, when Reverend Schipper's declining health and a diminishing need for refugee assistance resulted in its closure. By that time, Freedom Flight had been in operation for twenty-four years and had resettled more than eleven thousand refugees in West Michigan, not only from Southeast Asia but other parts of the world as well. The deaths of Reverend Schipper in 2006 and his wife in 2011 saddened the thousands of Vietnamese who came to the Grand Rapids area as a result of their compassion and devotion. After their arrival in the city, many of the Vietnamese had invited the Schippers to special celebrations of their families. There's probably no non-Vietnamese couple in America who has been to more Vietnamese weddings.

The life-changing efforts of Howard and Marybelle Schipper started out on an airplane awaiting takeoff in California—and ended up bringing joy to thousands of refugees and Americans whose ancestors had come to these shores many years earlier. *Author's collection.*

The Vietnamese Americans in Grand Rapids are grateful for the compassion of President Ford, too. As the war in Vietnam was nearing an end, he ordered American ships to assist in evacuating refugees. He also advocated resettling Vietnamese refugees in the United States.

Ron Nessen, his press secretary, later recalled Ford's reaction when he was shown a report that the House of Representatives had rejected a bill that would have provided funds for the resettlement of refugees from Vietnam. "I'd never heard Ford curse before," Nessen said, "but he did that day when he read the story."

Besides President Ford and the Schippers, hundreds of ordinary citizens in the Grand Rapids area reached out to the thousands of refugees who stepped off planes at the airport during the last decades of the twentieth century. Those people changed countless lives—not only of the newcomers but their own as well.

CHAPTER 18

Children of Dust

Among the last to fly out of Vietnam and into Grand Rapids were youngsters who may have had an even greater right to a new life in America than any of those who preceded them. Their mothers were Vietnamese, but their fathers were American GIs. They were called *Bui Doi*, the dust of life, and in Vietnam they were despised and were victims of discrimination.

And they might never have come to America, had it not been for a photographer, a school public relations aide, four teenagers and a congressman.

The photographer was Audrey Tiernan, who had gone to Ho Chi Minh City in October 1985 on assignment for the Long Island newspaper *Newsday*. There she met and photographed Le Van Minh, a polio-stricken, crippled boy who survived by begging and selling origami on the city's streets. He was able to move about only by crawling on all fours, and in the photo he was holding aloft a paper flower that he had made. It was an especially poignant picture.

A year after the photo appeared in *Newsday*, it was brought into a classroom at Huntington High School on Long Island, New York, by Gloria Blauvelt, a school district aide working in public relations. She was meeting with student-government leaders. Pointing to the picture, she said, "Bring him to America. Out of the billions of people in this world, this is one life we could save!"

Moved by the touching image and inspired by the challenge, four of the students—Susan Forte, Mario Sandler, Cara Scalia and David Zack—moved

Tuan Truong, one of the many Vietnamese Amerasians who flew to Grand Rapids, and his mother, Su, were among those who benefited from Bethany Christian Service's Amerasian Mentor Program. Tuan, who changed his name to Ryan when he became a U.S. citizen, had hardly gotten off the plane before he began intensive efforts to learn English. Two months after arrival, he entered Grand Rapids Community College; and a few years later, he received a degree in chemical engineering from Michigan State University. *Author's collection.*

into action. In less than six weeks, they collected twenty-seven thousand signatures on petitions to bring Minh to America. Then they turned to their congressman, Robert Mrazek, for help.

He was skeptical about the possibility of bringing Minh to America, but he agreed to at least consider the idea after one of the students told him, "You're quitting before you even start."

The enthusiasm of the quartet of teenagers was contagious, and Mrazek boarded a plane in June 1987 and soared across the Pacific to Vietnam. There he found Minh and cut through the red tape that made it possible for the boy to fly back to the United States with him.

While in Vietnam, the congressman saw many more Amerasians and was moved by their plight. Back in Washington, he proposed legislation that would make it possible for them to come to America. His Amerasian Homecoming Act was approved by Congress and signed into law by President Reagan before the end of 1987.

And that opened the door for more than twenty thousand additional Amerasians to come to the land of their fathers and to bring seventy-five thousand of their relatives with them. Mrazek pointed out that this wouldn't have been possible without the photo, the school's PR aide and, especially, the students.

Many of the Amerasians who flew to Grand Rapids with others of their families were without church sponsors to greet them when they arrived at Ford International Airport. However, Bethany Christian Services established an Amerasian Mentor Program that paired the newcomers with volunteers who guided and supported them as they adjusted to life in a strange new land.

Hundreds of lives were changed by this outreach—lives of Amerasians, of their Vietnamese relatives and of American mentors. And all of that happened because somebody took a picture, somebody showed it to the right people, four kids cared and a congressman responded in a big way.

Index

About the Author

In 1944 at the age of sixteen, Gordon Beld began writing sports for the *Grand Rapids Press*. Two years later, as a trooper of the U.S. Army's Constabulary in Germany, one of his duties was writing "66th Squadron News" for the *Constabulary Lightning Bolt*. After military service, he wrote for the *Grand Rapids Herald* for twelve years until the paper ceased publication. He then returned to the *Press* as a writer and copyreader for six years. During most of the years he wrote for the *Press* and *Herald*, he simultaneously taught English and history in suburban Grand Rapids schools. For twenty-four years, he was director of news services and publications at Alma College.

After retirement, he continued in the fields of education and journalism on a part-time basis as an academic advisor for Davenport College and writer for Grand Valley State University. During the first decade of the twenty-first century, he was a frequent contributor to *Michigan History* and *Grand Rapids* magazines. Besides hundreds of features on local and regional history, he is the author of *A Gentle Breeze from Gossamer Wings*, a historical novel published in 1999, and *Grand Times in Grand Rapids*, a 2012 release of The History Press. For more than thirty years, the principal interest of Gordon and his wife, Martha, has been to assist refugees and other immigrants in their adjustment to a new culture and language in America. They were involved with Cambodians when they lived in Alma, Vietnamese in Grand Rapids and Kosovars in Holland. For the past twenty-three years, Gordon has provided voluntary writing and photographic assistance to Exodus World Service, a Chicago-area agency whose mission is to link incoming refugees with caring Christians. He also assisted in an English-as-a-Second-Language class for immigrants in Holland for eight years. He holds degrees from Hope College and the University of Michigan.